"AOS GUERREIROS"

(Overleaf, pages 2-3) *A sergeant from the* Batalhão Especial de Fronteira *(BEF), the Special Border Battalion, flies over the northern Amazon border. Tension is always high when flying over the "Ocean of Trees."* **(Overleaf, pages 4-5)** *Students at* Centro de Instrução de Guerra na Sêlva *(CIGS), the Jungle Warfare Instruction Center, must learn how to capture, handle, and cook snakes. This boa constrictor would provide ample food.* **(Overleaf, pages 6-7)** Força Aérea Brasileira *(FAB), the Brazilian Air Force, uses the venerable C-130 Hercules to supply distant jungle garrisons. It can also be used for aerial refueling, for dropping paratroops, as a gunship, or as a hospital plane. In a region such as the Amazon, the sight of an FAB Hercules means relief for troops, Indians, and civilians.* **(Overleaf, pages 8-9)** *After springing from the Peruvian Andes on a long journey east, the Solimões River meets the Negro River just outside Manaus, where it assumes the name Amazonas. For almost 20 miles (30 kilometers), the black waters of the Negro and the caramel waters of the Solimões flow alongside each other without mixing.* Navio Patrulha Fluvial *(NaPaFlu), river patrol ship,* Pedro Teixeira *steams towards the "encounter of the waters," one of the wonders of the Amazon.* **(page 10)** *Yanomami children accept a gift of biscuits from a young FAB C-115 Buffalo pilot.* **(page 13)** *NaPaFlu* Raposo Tavares *passes through a small* paraná, *or river channel.* **(page 15)** *A young Marine Corps sergeant of the Amazon detachment.*

Foreword © 1992 by Vernon Walters. All rights reserved.
Designed by Alcemir José da Silva
Edited by Ross A. Howell Jr., Anne J. Douthat, and Claudia J. Garthwait.
Photographs © 1992 by Carlos Lorch. All rights reserved.
Text © 1992 by Carlos Lorch. All rights reserved.

Photos page 24 (Jaguar), page 25 (Boa, Squirrel Monkey) and page 103 (Navy Dental Surgeon) by Monica A.P. Lorch.

Special thanks: General Nialdo de Oliveira Bastos / General (Res) Carlos Olavo Guimarães / General Antenor de Santa Cruz Abreu / Major General Fernando Mendes Nogueira (FAB) / Major General Antônio Alberto de Toledo Lobato (FAB) / Comandante Ivan Pereira Areias (FLOTAM) / Colonel Gastão Puchalski Lopês / Colonel Adalberto Bueno da Cruz / Colonel Newton Bonumá dos Santos / Colonel Venancio Grossi (FAB) / Commander Evandro de Araújo Sobral Filho (FLOTAM) / Lt. Colonel Francisco Raul de Castro Lima França / Lt. Colonel Ivan Monteiro / Lt. Colonel Teomar Fonseca Quírico (FAB) / Lieutenant Commander (FN) Adauto Rocha De Lamare Leite / Major Luiz Fernandes de Oliveira (FAB) / Major Antonio Carlos Moretti Bermudez (FAB) / Mr. Piero Ruzzenenti / Mr. Raimundo Carlos Bezerra / Mr. Breno Lorch / Manoel Liduino / and especially to my wife, Monica, without whom this book would it have been possible.

Library of Congress Catalog Card Number 92-70129
ISBN 0-943231-48-5
Printed and bound in Hong Kong.

Published by Action Editora Ltda., Av. das Américas, 3333 s/817, Barra da Tijuca Riò de Janeiro, RJ, Brasil. CEP. 22.631, telephone (021) 325-7229, in conjunction with Howell Press, Inc., 1147 River Road, Bay 2, Charlottesville, VA 22901, telephone (804) 977-4006.

ACTION EDITORA / HOWELL PRESS

JUNGLE WARRIORS

DEFENDERS OF THE AMAZON

BANCO DO BRASIL

TEXT AND PHOTOGRAPHS BY CARLOS LORCH
FOREWORD BY VERNON WALTERS

CONTENTS

FOREWORD

By what one might call an accident of history, it fell to me to participate actively in the preparation and training of Brazilian troops for combat in the Italian theater of operations during World War II. I then served with the First Brazilian Infantry Division in combat in Italy for the 249 days that the division was engaged with the German Army.

Because I spoke Portuguese, I had been involved with the Brazilian Army in Brazil. Later, when I was sent to Italy, I served as the aide de camp to Lt. Gen. Mark Clark, Fifth Army commander. Upon the arrival of the Brazilian troops, I was designated by General Clark as his personal representative to the Brazilian Expeditionary Force. In that capacity I served until the end of the war at Gen. Mascarenhas de Moraes' command post.

Thus I had a most unusual opportunity to observe Brazilian soldiers in combat under geographic and climatic conditions that they had never faced before. It is therefore with great pleasure that I write this foreword to JUNGLE WARRIORS.

After the war I was assistant military attache in Brazil from 1945 to 1948. Fourteen years later, I returned to Brazil as the defense and army attache. During that posting I drove more than 60,000 miles (96,560 kilometers), visiting garrisons in the most remote parts of the country at a time when very few roads were paved. I drove from Rio de Janeiro to the Peruvian border in 1966. The journey took twenty-nine days in a four-wheel-drive, 3/4-ton truck. I drove from Brasilia to Belem while the road was still under construction. I sailed by river steamer down the Amazon from Manaus to Belem and down the Sao Francisco River by paddle-wheel steamer(built in Pittsburgh in 1865) from Pirapora to Joazeiro and Petrolina. I sailed up the Paraguay River from Asuncion, Paraguay, to Corumba in western Mato Grosso. On all of these trips I was aided by the Brazilian Army and visited a large number of their installations.

These journeys enabled me to see soldiers from all parts of Brazil, including the 50 percent of the country that is covered with what Americans would call "jungle."

The Brazilians call it "selva."

Until World War II Brazilians had thought strategically almost exclusively in terms of potential war with Argentina. Fortunately, that rivalry has since ebbed away. With its commitment in WWII, Brazil took its first step onto the world stage as something more than just a large regional power. Brazil comprises almost half the territory of the South American continent. It is nearly five times as large in population as the next most populated country in South America. It is different because its people speak Portuguese and not Spanish, and because it was fortunate enough to achieve independence in a single national entity.

Unlike most other nations on the continent it has no border quarrels; Brazil has negotiated peaceful settlements with all its neighbors. Its Army has been as much involved in nation building as the U.S. Army was in the nineteenth century when we reached across the North American continent to the Pacific.

Brazil has a highly professional Army, Navy, and Air Force. Most officers in positions of responsibility have not only graduated from their own schools of higher military learning, but from United States and major European military institutions, as well.

Brazilian troops participated in peace-keeping operations in the Middle East and in the Dominican Republic. In the latter case the Brazilian Air Force flew their contingent to the country, rotated the detachment several times, and kept their forces supplied. The immense size of the country and the paucity of ground infrastructure have imposed special responsibilities on the Air Force and Navy, who are in great part responsible for binding the country together.

Every year, the armed forces return to civilian life tens of thousands of soldiers who have learned to read and write in the olive green uniform of the Army. The Air Force handles most of the air-traffic control in the country, and the Navy handles many of the navigational map-making duties that are carried out in the U.S. by civilian branches of the federal govermment. In states like Amazonas there may be only one inhabitant per square mile; the frontiers are long and inaccessible, and drug trafficking has presented an enormous new challenge to Brazil.

The long, jungle-clad frontiers with Bolivia, Peru, Colombia, Venezuela, French Guiana, Surinam, and Guyana have imposed special requirements on the Brazilian armed forces. From these realities arose the decision to train "Jungle Warriors" on the ground in the middle of the "Sea of Trees," that is, in the midst of the Amazonian rain forest. Having driven through this vast forest for many days under the towering canopy of trees, I wonder at the reports of burning large parts of it. My experience was that it was either wet or dripping most of the time. It rains several times a day. There is no bridge across the Amazon River from its source to its mouth, in which lies the island of Marajo, which is larger than Switzerland. Brazil is a country in which nothing is small.

Even during the time the military played an important role in the government, the armed forces did not receive a large part of the national budget, far smaller in fact, in spite of the country's size, than in the United States or in most European countries.

Brazil has a conscript army in which the soldiers are drawn from all parts of the country. In the jungle areas, the soldiers are encouraged to settle down and start families after finishing their service in order to colonize the sparsely populated areas. In this tradition of soldiers' nation building, the foundation of a jungle training center comes naturally. Brazil knows that a great part of her destiny will be decided in the vast territories where the tree canopy seems endless.

Brazilians were very concerned some years ago when a book was published suggesting that countries with large areas and relatively small populations should open their lands to unlimited immigration. The idea turned Brazil's attention very much to the huge, relatively unpopulated northern part of the country and led to the setting up of a major new army headquarters in the Amazon and a redoubling of the nation-building efforts of some five battalions of engineers, charged with opening roads into the "Sea of Trees." One of these battalions in particular, the Fifth Engineer Construction Battalion, was my host on the twenty-nine-day drive from Rio to near the Peruvian border. Their commander, an unforgettable man, Lieutenant Colonel Weber, deeply believed that his children would live in another kind of Brazil because of what he and his men were doing in the Amazon area. He was right. They will live in a better Brazil. For years the presence of the Fifth Engineer Battalion was the presence of the Brazilian government in much of this vast area.

Now new challenges in the form of guerrillas, drug traffickers, smugglers, and terrorists have arisen. The Center for Jungle Warfare Training will enable Brazil to keep the area peaceful as it develops into the twenty-first century. For this they have brought British, American, French, Portuguese, and others with experience in these special skills to help them train Brazil's Jungle Warriors of tomorrow.

On the wall of the Presidential Palace in Brasilia, there is an inscription in golden letters of the words spoken by President Juscelino Kubitschek when he laid the first stone of the new capital: "Here on this high central plateau, in the midst of this loneliness that will tomorrow be the center of the great decisions of our national life, I have cast my eyes once again towards the tomorrow of my country, and I face that oncoming dawn with unbounded faith in its great destiny." This is the faith that motivates the soldiers of Brazil. I have seen those soldiers in combat; their sons will not let them down.

Vernon A. Walters
Lieutenant General, U.S. Army (Ret)

(Previous spread) *Navy Esquilo pilots approach NaPaFlu Pedro Teixeira. This large ship serves as a forward platform for Navy helicopters and is capable of considerable firepower and flexibility.* **(Facing Page)** *Jungle Troops train near the Colombian border.* **(Left)** *CIGS troops on river warfare drill.*

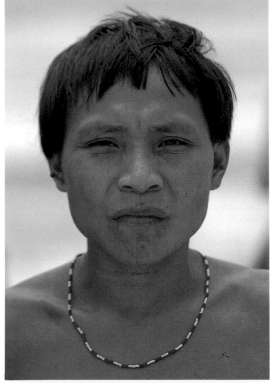

The Amazon jungle is perhaps the last truly wild frontier on earth.

THE JUNGLE

The Last Wild Place

Few places create as much fear in the human mind as the jungle. An impenetrable labyrinth of living matter in all stages of growth and decay, the jungle evokes the most primal sensations. There is no other region on earth more hostile and alien to man, both physically and psychologically.

The Amazon region of South America contains about one-third of all tropical jungle on the globe. It is a seemingly endless expanse of forest cut by one of the most massive river systems in existence. Any description of the vast Amazon region must refer to size and proportion. One can fit seventeen Vietnams, North and South, in the Brazilian Amazon territory alone, although the rain forest lies in the territory of seven countries. It is in Brazil, however, where most of the jungle is located, and where most interest is concentrated.

Brazil has over 2,000,000 square miles (5,600,000 square kilometers) of Amazon jungle, an area comprising roughly two-thirds of its territory, or an area the size of all Europe, excluding Russia. Brazil's armed forces must patrol some 7,000 miles (11,500 kilometers) of jungle border, roughly the equivalent of the northern border of the United States coast to coast. With incredible amounts of annual rainfall measuring from 50 to 120 inches (130 to 305 centimeters), the Amazon has not only developed an "ocean of trees" that can reach heights of over 130 feet (40 meters), but also the widest variety of plant and animal life anywhere on earth.

The Amazon River basin spreads over forty-five percent of Brazil's territory. Its major river, the Amazonas, runs close to 4,000 miles (6,400 kilometers) from the Andes Mountains to the Atlantic Ocean, a distance greater than the distance between New York and San Francisco. It is the volume of water carried by the Amazon, however, that is truly impressive. It would take the Nile, Yangtze, and Mississippi rivers combined to equal the flow of water

the Amazon takes to the sea. Reaching a width of 6 miles (10 kilometers), with its mouth measuring over 85 miles (140 kilometers), the Amazon can cause incredible tidal bores that reach a height of over 12 feet (3.5 meters). It is easy to see why it is almost impossible to refer to the Amazon without using superlatives. Such a vast region has, however, Brazil's lowest population density, with about one person per square mile (2.6 per square kilometer), making it one of the last truly wild places on earth.

In the last few years, attention has been focused on this long-forgotten region. Under its giant forest canopy, the Amazon jungle contains large deposits of important minerals such as iron ore, gold, diamonds, uranium, tin ore, niobium, and others. Slowly but consistently, Brazil has been trying to develop the region, building roads, power plants, airfields, and settlements. The inhabitants of the Amazon are mainly poor, undernourished families unable to find alternative ways of making a living in a society long accustomed to existing off what the river and the jungle provide. With these people in mind, Brazil has been fighting to bring progress into the region.

In the early eighties, the notion of the destruction of the rain forest became an important topic for discussion all over the world. Accusations that Brazil was turning the rain forest into a desert, and affecting the ozone layer in the atmosphere suddenly made the region an item of media interest. Slowly it was learned that although the crop-clearing fires typical of the region are by no means healthy, most of the pollution and its by-products affecting the planet today come primarily from the burning of fossil fuels. Brazil has shown the world that of all the carbon dioxide emitted in the atmosphere, it is responsible for no more than 5%, while industrialized nations of the northern hemisphere let out much greater amounts. The United States alone for example, is responsible for nearly twenty-three percent of all carbon dioxide emissions into the atmosphere.

Deep in the hot, humid, and oppressive "Green Hell," untrained men can easily lose control.

The notion that the Amazon jungle is the "lungs of the planet" has also been proven false, as the rain forest has been shown to consume all of the oxygen that it produces in a clear sign of perfect natural balance. Even though the Amazon "scare" seems to be coming to rational terms, the Brazilian government is on top of the issue to ensure that the Amazon's development is carried through in a planned and environmentally friendly manner.

While international controversy in the eighties swirled around environmental issues related to the Amazonian rain forest, there have been other threats to the region that have required the attention of Brazil's armed forces. Crack-downs on Colombian, Peruvian, and Bolivian drug cartels have rerouted part of the international drug trade through Brazilian territory along the Amazon on a looping route to Europe and the eastern United States. Guerrilla groups from neighboring countries seek occasional safe havens across the border when things get hot, and gold and diamond miners have turned large parts of the region into a twentieth-century version of the American "Wild West," including conflicts with native Indians. In addition

to policing these situations, Brazil's military provides human-itarian aid to the inhabitants of remote and isolated reaches of the jungle, along with guaranteeing the integrity of the country's borders.

These tasks are as formidable as the Amazon region itself.

Inside the Green Hell

Each breath comes as a shallow draw. It seems as if nothing I do can pull enough air into my lungs. Sweat drips from the tip of my nose, but I have long given up on wiping it dry. Even the insects and leaves that brush against my face I now accept as part of my existence. The pack I carry adds to the weight of my sweat-drenched clothes and with every step increases my discomfort.

Our group has been off the small road we used to enter the jungle just forty-five minutes and I am already having a hard time keeping up. The feeling is one of sprint-ing in a sauna with my nose clogged. With every step, my boots dig into the rotten maze of thick, organic slime

that collects on the forest floor. The lower legs of my pants are filled with leaves and small furry spiders that are attached to the debris. Thick vines seem to reach out from the jungle floor like forearms grabbing at my ankles, and long wicked spines hang by the hundreds on every nearby tree. The terrain is very steep. Any flat area serves as a trough for the inevitable creek running through it.

In the Amazon you are always wet, from sweat, from the rivers, from the rain. It is a world of ninety-nine percent humidity. Blood pressure soars under the heat and thirst is never quenched. The tricks my mind is playing make everything worse. I lift my head to look ahead, but I can see no farther than sixty feet. My eyes have a hard time focusing. Everywhere I look seems the same—I have no sense of direction. Each step is a struggle. From time to time a huge log lies fallen ahead of us. Crossing one of them my foot caves in, and out of the rotten wood emerge hundreds of small, white larvae, squirming all over the dead trunk.

I know that snakes, scorpions, centipedes and a myriad other creatures lurk unseen around us, but my mind can no longer think about the possibility of an encounter.

The Jungle Warrior learns to turn the jungle into an ally. **(Facing page)** A marine drinks from a water vine. **(This page)** Capt. Francisco Ronald Rocha Fernandes, a CIGS instructor, navigates through dense jungle.

I am just too beat. The hunching up and down to bypass low branches and squeezing between the trunks of trees brings a sharp pain in the lower part of my spine. My breathing now comes in gasps. A sharp bell starts to ring in my ears. I stop, take a few deep breaths, a swig of water, and it's back on the path. I look up in a 180-degree arc overhead. Small blotches of blue signal the sky is above, but that is all I can see of it. All around me it is green. The forest seems to engulf everything that dares enter it, draining energy from any living thing. I wonder how men can spend weeks, months, and sometimes years in the jungle. How hard it would be not to go crazy. I try to think of something else, but it is impossible. My body feels as if it is rotting along with the trees and the leaves around it. Now I understand why the jungle has been called "The Green Hell."

I know for sure I would never find my way out on my own. Yet the men I am with are smiling and joking. Except for their boots and their sweat-drenched fatigues, they are immaculately clean. The ground seems flat and solid under their slow, rhythmic strides. The machete swings with an expert hand in a constant pendulum as if each arc gathered strength from the one before, and the jungle seems to open up before us. The thick barrel I have been staring at for the last fifty minutes dangles from the shoulder in front of me where the shotgun fits snugly.

"Here, look at this," says Capt. Francisco Ronald Rocha Fernandes from up ahead. "This is the *sapopemba,* the drum of the jungle." He is pointing to a huge tree,

whose roots reach from under it like giant tentacles. He pulls out his jungle knife and proceeds to beat on the side of the root. Suddenly, the jungle is filled with his thunder. "You can use this tree to communicate or to help someone locate you in the jungle." I stare blankly and store the information somewhere in the back of my mind.

"And this", says Capt. Edilson de Andrade Martini, with his constant smile, "is *breu preto,*" a sticky black tar hanging from the bark of a tree. "This we use to make fire," he says. "Come over here." I stumble to his side. He collects the sticky putty and rolls it into a marble-sized ball. As he lights it, a large flame engulfs the black stuff and burns on and on. "This," he says, "can really change your life in here."

After this diversion, we move on, a step at a time, in slow, regular movements. I cannot quite walk as they do, but I try my best to do so. I feel like throwing myself into a cool pool of water, but we are still on our way into the survival area. I count my steps, one... two... three.... one. Three steps represent a meter. Counting helps to ease the psychological drain, but I learn later that it is to be avoided at all costs on jungle patrols. Soon, I am so intent on the path and my counting that I never get beyond counting nineteen meters.

Moving in the jungle can have a hypnotic effect upon troops. The split second it would take them to react is crucial in jungle combat. Life depends on staying alert. We march on. A "klick" an hour, I am told, is the average speed for fit men in the jungle. I try hard not to lag behind.

"Let me show you something," grins Captain Ronald

during another pause for physical and psychological rest. "I will move away and you try to see me." I count his steps,... seven... eight... nine... invisible! I squint hard in every direction. He is nowhere to be seen. I try listening. Nothing. Suddenly, just as he left, he reappears. "I was never more than fifteen meters away," he says. In the jungle, untrained eyes go rapidly blind.

These small demonstrations take my mind away from the trek and before I know it we have reached our objective. Captain Martini explains that several groups of students have been dropped off in the jungle by their respective instructors. They are in the jungle survival phase of their training. They have been in the jungle for over seventy-two hours and don't know that they will be "rescued" in two more days.

We begin to see signs of their presence. A path has been cordoned off with vine and a small field latrine has been built with wood and straw. It is clean and sturdy. Up on a knoll, a small shelter on stilts is raised above the jungle floor. A flat log platform makes for a comfortable area beneath dry palm leaves. The ground around the shelter has been brushed clean and a low fire burns off to one side, protected from the wind and rain by a tall wall of intertwined leaves. The students have managed to create a bit of comfort in the jungle. Captain Martini informs me that these men were provided with just the essentials: one shotgun for hunting, a rifle for protection, six matches, a flashlight, one canteen each, and a jungle knife. In seventy-two hours, they had applied what they learned and turned the jungle into an ally.

On a small stool the students had built are the objects that will prove to their instructor how they managed to survive— the skin of a *jararaca* snake, one of the most poisonous; the carcass of a turtle, along with the shells of its eggs; dried husks of heart of palm; and the seeds and stems of fruits found and eaten. While the students look exhausted and gaunt, they have been more than able to take care of themselves. After inspecting the area, we move out. The path is every bit as demanding, requiring strength from deep within. But somehow, a portion of the weight has been taken off me. I know I am in good company.

Jungle Warriors

Brazil places much importance on its jungle troops. With two-thirds of its territory covered by thick, primary jungle, and the greatest potential for confrontation and conflict lying in its northern region, Brazil must field effective jungle-trained soldiers. These men not only learn the intricacies of befriending the jungle but also play an active part in the defense and integration of Brazil's Amazon region. They are the picket fence that must bar any threat to Brazil's integrity.

Occupying an area only recently reached by outposts of civilization, these troops perform dangerous and critical missions, be it the control of narcotics routes in support of federal police, the extraction of illegal gold prospectors, the protection of the Indians, or the supply of hard-to-reach villages and settlements. Once you have gone into the jungle with these men, you learn that "The Green Hell' can be dealt with. These men seem at home in the jungle; they seem to draw a primal energy from the rain forest. They are Brazil's "Jungle Warriors."

Stealth and ingenuity separate the hunter from the prey in the rain forest. **(This page)** *A BEF trooper hides and listens, sometimes for an hour if necessary, before making his next move.* **(Facing page)** *Mirrors and smoke can be used to signal to aircraft above the canopy.*

31

EARNING THE JAGUAR

The Most Frightening Battlefield

Through history, technology has been used to minimize the effects of terrain and weather upon troops at war. The Gulf War of 1991 saw advanced "smart" weapons used successfully to reduce Allied casualties, as well as to inflict enormous damage on Iraqi troops and strategic targets. In the jungle, however, technology has had little impact on warfare, and more conventional weapons and tactics must be employed.

Although wars have been fought in jungle terrain since ancient times, it was during the First World War that the concept of jungle warfare as we understand it today was introduced. In German East Africa (now Tanzania), the German Imperial Army, led by Gen. Paul von Lettow-Vorbeck, devised wildly unconventional guerrilla tactics for use against far superior British forces. Using well-trained native soldiers, taking refuge from pursuit in the jungle or over the border in the Portuguese colony of Mozambique, and employing hit-and-run tactics aimed at disrupting the British command and supply networks, General von Lettow-Vorbeck laid the foundations for future jungle conflicts. Never defeated, he surrendered in 1918 only after learning of Germany's capitulation in Europe. By understanding and using the jungle to his advantage, General von Lettow-Vorbeck rewrote the military strategy books of the period.

World War II saw the first large deployment of troops in jungle combat, and much of today's knowledge was tempered in the blood of that conflict. Idyllic atolls and South Pacific islands became tropical hells for U.S. Marines, GIs, and Japanese Imperial troops. Disease, hunger, torrential rains, and dense jungle caught both defender and attacker unprepared. Tarawa, Bougainville, and Guadalcanal were places where jungle warfare was learned in savage and fearsome ways.

Allied forces in Port Moresby, New Guinea, were separated from the Japanese in Rabaul by densely jungled mountain ranges. In a Japanese thrust over the central Owen Stanley Mountains, a single Australian battalion held off a Japanese advance of several thousand men for more than three months before falling back. After the battle for Port Moresby, the Japanese were forced to retreat through the jungle and were decimated as much by disease and hunger as by attacks from pursuing Allied troops. What became more and more apparent was man's ineptitude at waging war in the tropical rain forest.

About the formidable Burmese jungle of Southeast Asia, Winston Churchill wrote, "I disliked intensely the prospect of a large-scale campaign in northern Burma. One could not choose a worse place for fighting the Japanese." Yet the Burma Road was built, under terrible pressure to link Allied forces in India to Chiang Kai-Shek's troops in China. Like General von Lettow-Vorbeck before them, two men took the art of fighting in the jungle a step further. British General Orde Wingate's Chindits and American Frank Merrill's Marauders turned the tide of battle and shattered the myth of Japanese invincibility in the jungle. Slowly, the Allied troops succeeded in pushing the Japanese back over Burma. In the Battle of Imphal alone, the Japanese lost 65,000 men.

After World War II came the wars of colonial independence. Many nations, primarily in Asia and Africa, fought to oust the colonial powers from their territories. The first significant jungle confrontation of the period involved the French in Indochina against the Viet Minh. Through sustained control of the jungle and an effective supply system invisible to aerial reconnaissance, the Vietnamese were able to defeat the French colonial army, which stuck to roads, villages, forts, and airfields that were both predictable and vulnerable. In the battle of Dien Bien Phu, a crack garrison of paratroopers, French foreign legion

(**Previous spread**) *Students go through a gruelling nine weeks to earn the "Jaguar" at CIGS.* (**Facing page**) *Enter these gates and you are in Jungle Warrior country.* (**Above**) *Rappelling techniques are used to carry wounded safely and rapidly. The rappelling wall at CIGS offers an example of the harsh erosion that takes place in the Amazon.*

troops, and regular units of the French army were surrounded and torn apart by a superior Viet Minh army with a better understanding of jungle warfare tactics.

Further south, the British were facing a Communist-led insurgency in Malaya. Although the Chinese-backed guerrillas were well-organized, the British army tested innovative methods that were to prove extremely successful. Rather than attempt to enter territory in remote jungle-covered areas of the country, it devised a strategy to harass and destroy the guerrillas with their own brand of warfare. Special troops, mostly SAS (Special Air Service) and Gurkhas, honed their skills in small-group tactics and night fighting. A large-scale intelligence network was set up over the country and small units were sent into the bush on search-and-destroy missions. The population was the focus of a strong "hearts-and-minds" campaign aimed at denying the Communists support. Encounters were few and far

between, but sufficient to push the guerrillas gradually into the jungle. In most cases, the British were fighting with small, extremely well-trained squads, similar to those they were facing. Air support was available and intelligence was taken very seriously. With clever and pragmatic tactics, the British were successful in retaking the interior and virtually eliminating the insurgency in Malaya.

In the Caribbean, Fidel Castro's guerrillas hid in bases above Cuba's Sierra Maestra mountains using the jungle to hide and to prepare raids that slowly took their toll on the island's government.

Some of the ideas and tactics learned from these conflicts were studied and applied in Vietnam by U.S. Army Special Forces and Navy Seals. Although the American army fought mostly set battles against experienced, jungle-smart North Vietnamese and Viet Cong troops who wisely employed hit-and-run tactics, U.S. Army Special

(Top and bottom) *All rivers lead to larger rivers, then to the Amazon — this is one of the first lessons of survival in the Amazon basin. For practice in river tactics, students rub the reddish "tabatinga" clay onto their shirts and pants to seal small holes and seams. Special flotation devices are prepared to protect equipment.*

Forces effectively took the war to the enemy on its own terms. The Vietnamese, however, introduced a series of innovative techniques early on in the conflict, extracting from the jungle what their limited technology could not provide. Primitive but ingenious and effective traps, tunnel systems, camouflage covers, signals, and methods of navigation more than made up for the Viet Cong shortage of advanced weapons, although these became more plentiful as the war progressed.

In Africa, several conflicts raged during the same period, with guerrillas inspired by the Marxist rhetoric of Mao

Tse Tung, Ho Chi Minh, and Ernesto "Che" Guevara emerging from the jungle to strike against the colonial armies. In Rhodesia (now Zimbabwe), the government formed the elite Selous Scouts, who employed tactics used by the British in Malaya until political will ended the war. In Angola and Mozambique, the Portuguese fought insurgents of the UNITA (National Union for Total Independence of Angola), MPLA (Popular Movement for the Liberation of Angola) and FRELIMO (Mozambique Liberation Front) movements, learning gradually to drive deeper into the jungle. Were it not for the April 25, 1974, coup at home and diminishing

A CIGS patrol wades across an igarapé, or river tributary. The point man carries a shotgun, commonly used in the jungle to cover wide areas during fast and intense firefights.

world support, the Portuguese might have controlled the rebel forces.

Today, war is a possibility in every jungle area on the globe. Central America echoes with the rattle of machine gun fire from Guatemala and El Salvador to Nicaragua. Panama cannot be ruled out as a potential war zone. The whole of Southeast Asia is heavily armed, with Vietnam playing a strong role and possessing a large jungle-capable army, not to mention the battle-hardened Khmer Rouge of Cambodia and the large private armies of Thai and Laotian heroin and opium dealers in the golden triangle. Africa remains volatile. South America's jungles sometimes witness large confrontations between drug traffickers, guerrilla groups, and military forces.

With one of the largest jungle regions in the world to defend, Brazil has developed perhaps the most demanding and significant jungle warfare school in existence. It is known as *Centro de Instrução de Guerra na Selva* (CIGS), the Center for Jungle Warfare Instruction. Here

a special type of warrior is trained, one who is at home in what is perhaps the most frightening battlefield of all.

Home of the Jungle Warrior

The first thing I notice as we drive to the CIGS gates is the large symbol of the jaguar head on the wall of the compound. A sentry looks over our vehicle from a tall, straw-covered observation post. The gates open, and as we drive past, the nine guards bellow in one voice, *"SELVA!,"* Portuguese for "jungle." A long road leads to the main buildings in the distance through dense jungle on both sides. The unit's mascots, fully grown black and spotted jaguars, roam freely inside the compound.

At CIGS, *"Selva!"* is everything. "Understood" is *"Selva!"* "Yes sir" is *"Selva!"* "Good morning" is *"Selva!"* Even "You're welcome" is *"Selva!"* Every aspect of the program at CIGS serves to remind the participants that the jungle is ever present, the reason they have come.

CIGS is located in Manaus, close to the center of the Amazon, on the banks of the Negro River. The first challenge is the weather: hot and horribly muggy. The body goes into low gear and the mind seems to wander. It takes fifteen days to become acclimated, and at CIGS this is done through heavy running and exercising. Next come the actual tests, ranging from health examinations to long-distance swimming in the river. No man unfit will be allowed on the course, for he can be dangerous to himself as well as to his fellow students. At CIGS, a student will be transformed from urban dweller into a Jungle Warrior, both in body and mind.

Qualifying for the course is one of the toughest tests in any army, anywhere. At the begining of each period, a percentage of hopefuls has to absorb the shock of rejection. Since only volunteers can take the CIGS course for officers and NCOs, rejection comes as a major disappointment. However, at CIGS, they prefer to have their students disappointed rather than dead.

The course usually begins with thorough instruction about what to expect from the jungle. Information about hunting, fishing, preparing simple traps, and using resources available in the jungle for food, shelter, fire, and medicine is included, always with the assurance that everything that is being taught can be found in abundance in the training area. How to cope with tropical diseases and dangerous animals is also stressed. Slowly, the students prepare to face the jungle in what will probably be the greatest test of their lives.

The initial phase takes place in the jungle training areas, in dark, frightening, primary jungle a few hours outside Manaus. The students take classes where they learn to identify the resources of the rain forest. The variety is unbelievable. Several fruits grow wild, from pineapple, passion fruit, and *jambo* (also known as malay apple), to guava, *graviola* (also known as *cherimoya*), breadfruit, *tucumã,* apricot, *buriti,* coconuts, *cupuaçu,* and *ingá,* a string-bean-like stem filled with furry white balls that are cool and sweet to the tongue. Several types of nuts are abundant in the forest. They are a primary source of energy, as is heart of palm, or the water-diluted sap of several trees, such as the *sorveira* and the *amapá,* affectionately called "the cow trees."

Hunting and trapping, essential skills in the jungle, are taught to perfection. Students learn to build traps with nothing more than a knife, twigs, branches, and vines. Spears are made for hunting and fishing. Vines become ropes, and dry leaves and straw are transformed into roofs and walls. Certain woods, such as ironwood, are ideal for shelters, while others are ideal for rafts and floating devices. Even a special ash found in certain trees serves a purpose — when lit, it burns for relatively long periods.

Since fire can be man's best friend in the jungle — for cooking, keeping predators at bay, making weapons and tools, signaling, or providing light and heat at night — making and tending fires is taught to exhaustion. Medicines are identified, as are symptoms of common diseases such as leishmaniosis, malaria, typhoid fever, tetanus, yellow fever, and cholera.

Snakes are a serious topic for study because they represent both life and death for the students. Serpents are plentiful in the jungle, representing an important food source. But many highly poisonous types inhabit the Amazon, including the *jararaca, surucucu pico de jaca,* and coral snake, and they must be recognized and handled with extreme care. Students learn that poisonous snakes can be of two kinds, with different venoms. Some possess neurotoxins which affect the brain and nervous system, causing difficulty in breathing and swallowing, finally disrupting heartbeat. Others possess hemotoxins which damage blood vessels and body tissues.

Non-venomous snakes, like the anaconda *(sucuri)* and the boa constrictor *(jibóia),* are also abundant. Although they carry no venom and are slower than their cousins with fangs, these snakes kill their prey through asphyxiation, then swallow it whole. Anacondas can measure up to 30 feet (10 meters) and are particularly dangerous in the water. I asked one of the CIGS's top instructors what scared him most in the jungle. "Meeting a *sucuri* in the water," was his quick reply.

Water is abundant in the jungle, if not from creeks and tributaries, called *igarapés,* then from leaves that collect dew, or from water vines, coarse branches that gush streams of fresh water when cut with a machete. Certain leaves can be used to make teas that soothe diarrhea, cramps, and fever. For fire, certain trees ooze a type of pitch. Black pitch ignites easily and burns for a long time. White pitch, similar to paraffin, is ideal for makeshift candles. Special vines and large leaves are used to build the *rabo de jacu,* a weather wall that will protect a fire from wind and rain. White straw, in reality the underside of the *babaçu* leaf that has a light fluorescent glow at night, is used for signaling or marking the direction of a path.

After extensive training, students go into the jungle by themselves for their survival trials. They are subjected to gruelling time schedules, very little sleep, and constant surprises in order to simulate battle pressure. Groups of six to eight men are led into the jungle, with nothing but the most essential equipment. They remain for several days. This stage of the course follows the old CIGS adage, "When in the jungle, you must learn to become the hunter. Otherwise, you will become the prey."

For many of these students, even the successful ones,

Traps were often used by the Vietnamese against the French and American armies in Southeast Asia. They can be simple, such as a grenade in a can; complex, such as the "death flight" onto pointed punji sticks; or ingenious, such as a rifle triggered by a trip wire.

The jungle provides just about everything to the experienced Jungle Warrior. **(Above)** Here, a display is prepared to introduce students to types of food that can be found in the jungle. **(Facing page)** A path is marked on the jungle floor with "white straw" from the babaçu tree.

the nights on survival course will be the worst of their lives. Lt. Col. Paulo César Freitas de Oliveira, the commanding officer of the First BIS, one of the most important operational jungle battalions told me, "When I went through the survival stage of my course, an Argentine student lost 24 kilos (50 pounds). I myself lost eight (18 pounds)."

Although the men hunt, gather, and eat what they can find, the pressure is intense, both physically and psychologically. After completing CIGS survival training, however, officers will lose their fear of the jungle. They learn to identify it as a provider, as long as they use their brains, their cool, and their knowledge. An old saying puts it well: "The jungle does not belong to the strongest. It belongs to the most skillful, the most resistent, and the most sober."

After a few days alone in the jungle, the groups are "rescued." They begin to ready themselves for the next stages of the course, but not before being treated to a well-balanced meal.

Students may quit the course at any time, and some do. Such action is not registered in their individual military files, since the CIGS course is voluntary and its toughness legendary. On many occasions during the course, in fact, CIGS instructors will tempt students with offers of safe

return to civilization, hot meals, clean beds, and other comforts. Psychological pressure never slackens, although it is clear that the instructors always are concerned with the safety and welfare of their students. Each of these jungle-hardened instructors has undergone the CIGS course and knows exactly what these students are experiencing. Silently inside, each of these men is pushing the students on, hoping that they too will be able to become Jungle Warriors.

The most important lesson in the survival doctrine concerns the vast river system. There are more than 10,000 miles (16,000 kilometers) of waterway that run toward the sea. Each river eventually flows into the Amazonas, where population centers and river boats are abundant. Besides being able to survive and navigate on land, therefore, the Jungle Warrior must be proficient in his knowledge of the rivers of the region.

The aquatic stage of the course deals with offensive and defensive use of the rivers. Everything, from river combat tactics and the building and use of floating devices and rafts to silent infiltration and extraction techniques using fast-moving boats, is studied until it becomes second nature. Sticks of wood can be strung together for flotation.

River operations are practiced intensively at CIGS.

Empty canteens, secured with a belt, make a good life jacket. With neither canteens nor a belt, the reddish-brown clay on the banks of most rivers,

called *tabatinga,* can be rubbed on trousers or fatigue shirts to seal any seams or openings. Tying off the trousers or shirt in a special way will create a cushion of air that enables an individual to float for long distances. If tools and time are available, substantial rafts can be built, as well as dugout log canoes, which can easily reach populated areas.

Infiltration training is of extreme importance, as the rivers are the fastest surface route to reach an objective. Rubber boats, local dugouts, fiberglass assault boats, and even old river boats are used for this training. Methods to protect weapons from water, special ways to lace shoe-strings for quick release of boots, and a series of other tecniques are learned at this stage.

From Prey to Hunters

CIGS students have now progressed from being survivors to the point where they can fight in the jungle. Navigation, communication, operations with aircraft, small squad tactics, the use and maintenance of different weapons, preparation of positions, camouflage and ambush techniques, traps and barriers, and above all, pressure, take the students into the combat stage of the course. After long marches, students are asked to assemble different weapons that are dismantled, the several parts thrown together in a box. The time period given is far too short to accomplish the task. The objective is to evaluate the student's response to stress.

Traversing obstacles is extremely important in this stage of the course. The estimated speed of a combat group moving in the jungle is about 3,200 feet (roughly 1,000 meters) per hour for fit men, and 990 feet (roughly

In the jungle any weapon is an advantage. These crossbows,
developed at CIGS, can shoot up to five arrows simultaneously.
Their tips are dipped in excrement or curare.

Navigation in the jungle is one of the most difficult arts to master. The sun and the stars can rarely be used, as they cannot be seen from under the dense jungle canopy. Map and compass are essential. Practically every exercise requires that a squad open up a path through the jungle to a specific objective. Taking a straight line to the target is not always possible, so perfect interpretation of position is imperative at all times. A common blunder occurs when a squad comes upon an already existent trail leading in the same direction as its objective. Man's instincts can take over. Rather than follow the correct azimuth drawn by the initial plan, the squad will follow the trail, sometimes ending up very far from their objective. Without initial coordinates, a squad can easily become completely lost. Col. Adalberto Bueno da Cruz, an ex-commander at CIGS, says, "It is quite common to leave behind the azimuth and get seduced by a trail. We call that 'following the trailuth'."

Communications are also difficult, as the canopy tends to block out radio transmissions in most parts of the jungle. Signal communications using smoke, light, or mirrors are of little use, since visibility inside the forest is so limited. The rapid climbing of trees, known as *peconha,* uses ropes or a special type of leaf woven into a sling to resolve the communications problem, and also provides a way to collect fruits and eggs. Once atop the canopy, radio aerials can be put to work and aircraft or boats can be contacted with the usual signal communications.

Aircraft are very important in jungle warfare, not only for the fast supply of equipment but also for the insertion and extraction of combat troops, wounded, and supplies. Were it not for the excellent use of medevac helicopters in Vietnam, U.S. casualties would have been far higher. *Força Aérea Brasileira* (FAB) helicopters and transports operate extensively with CIGS courses, supplying student groups with everything from parachute-landed cargo to makeshift poncho parachutes for light deliveries. Drop zone coordination, signaling, and even forward air control exercises are conducted. Helicopters carry in assault troops or special forces units that rappel down ropes. Insertion also occurs through helo-casting techniques. At low hover, choppers offload troops who jump fully-equipped into a river and swim to shore. Rapid extraction using McGuire rigs is also practiced.

Traps and ambushes are a very important part of small squad training. Although many of the techniques were adapted from original Vietnamese traps, most were conceived by experts at CIGS. Traps such as the "Malayan hat," a large wooden box holding thick downward-pointing spikes, can be left dangling by a rope or vine over a trail, well-camouflaged by foliage until some unfortunate

300 meters) per hour for a squad carrying a wounded comrade. Terrain in the Amazon is not flat, and the ability to surpass vertical obstacles is essential. Individual climbs and descents using rappelling techniques, as well as transport of wounded comrades, are trained to perfection.

At CIGS, pressure is applied at all times to the students, although it is clear that the instructors are always concerned with their safety and well-being.

Several countries send students to CIGS. Here, a Brazilian instructor explains the uses of the "white straw" to students from the **(left to right)** French foreign legion, Argentine Commandos, Ecuadoran Special Forces, French Infanterie de Marine, U.S. Army Special Forces, and Surinam Special Forces.

The jungle trap course at CIGS is impressive. Students are taught how to make traps out of native jungle wood, vines, roots, and leaves. I was shown more than twenty different traps, each with harrowing characteristics. One, a bridge over a large tributary, seemed to provide easy passage to the far bank. Halfway or so across, however, the bridge contained a horrible surprise. A small section of its stick floor was loose. It was almost impossible for a person to cross without the bottom giving way. The plunge was not only into water but onto *punji* sticks hidden beneath the river's surface. Students are trained not only in setting traps for animals and the enemy, but also in identifying ideal locations and telltale signs of enemy barriers and traps. Students at CIGS will ultimately be leading Brazil's Jungle Warriors into the forest, and they must remember to think like the hunter rather than the prey.

Other weapons and tactics taught at CIGS are those used by Brazil's native Indians. Many instructors at CIGS are experts with blowguns, bows and arrows, and machetes. From the bows and arrows, modern, functional crossbows have been adapted for use in the jungle for silent combat in the bush. Poisons and their antidotes, used by tribes against animals and human enemies, are also identified at CIGS and passed on from one generation to the next.

To the Jungles of the World

CIGS accepts students not only from Brazil's army, air force, and marines, but also from the armed forces of other countries. These foreign officers must learn Portuguese and participate in groups with Brazilian students. Many of Brazil's Latin American neighbors such as Colombia, Ecuador, Peru, Venezuela, Guyana, Surinam, Uruguay, Argentina, Paraguay, and Bolivia send students to the CIGS courses on a regular basis. Most of these countries have large expanses of jungle-covered terrain; they send officers to CIGS to receive instructor training and to refine techniques and knowledge. At a recent course, I had the opportunity to talk to a young Argentine commando lieutenant. For him, the chance to take the course at CIGS had been a reward from the Argentine army. He had placed first in his country's commando course, a tough, all-aspect drill, and had been sent to CIGS for more advanced jungle training.

Many European countries send students to CIGS. France takes its strategic possesion of French Guiana very seriously, especially since that is where the Kourou Space Center launches the highly successful *Ariane* rocket. Ninety percent of French Guiana is jungle, defended by elite foreign legion and *Infanterie de Marine* troops.

"I was sent here so that after finishing the course

soul breaks the trip wire. Such traps can kill, yet more importantly, they can cause panic in an enemy patrol. Holes, trenches, and pits in the ground can be concealed with undergrowth, hiding excrement-covered *punji* sticks. These "death traps," built to inflict terrible pain or death, also undermine enemy morale. In the jungle a flesh wound can rapidly become infected, causing terrible pain and psychological stress.

(Top) *A young French army captain eats the* tapuru, *a coconut-tasting larva found in the* babacu *tree.* (Bottom left) *A student from Ecuador on the obstacle course.* (Above) *An Argentine commando fires an FAL rifle.*

(Top) *Traps are thoroughly studied by foreign students.*
(Bottom) *A Student from Guyana practices hunting techniques. Note the flashlight on the stock used to temporarily blind the prey.* **(Above)** *Legionnaires are frequent students at CIGS.*

I could become an instructor at our jungle course in Guyana," says a tough-looking legionnaire captain selected for the CIGS course. "We hear that the course is very hard, very tough," adds a young *Infanterie de Marine* officer with jungle training in Gabon. Many students and visitors are combat veterans who bring special techniques that add to the curriculum at CIGS. Portuguese army officers whose army acquired extensive knowledge in Africa and British SAS officers with extensive training in southeast Asia and the Falklands have brought specific tips that have been rapidly absorbed and applied at CIGS. The school is not only a disseminator of information but also a forum for Jungle Warriors from all over the world.

The sixties and seventies found U.S. troops in the jungles of Vietnam, Laos, and Cambodia. In the eighties the jungles of Grenada and Central America saw limited fighting by U.S. forces as well as the presence of Special Forces advisers. In the nineties, especially after the invasion of Panama in which there was some jungle fighting, there is concern that Americans will see combat in the northern territory of South America. The U.S. Army faces growing threats from narco-terrorists, especially in Colombia and Peru. At CIGS techniques of jungle warfare will be learned and tested by a few hand-picked American students from U.S. Army Special Forces and other units.

The U.S. Army has a jungle warfare school at Fort Sherman, Panama, that along with CIGS and a few other smaller jungle warfare centers attracts the attention of jungle warfare communities around the world. I asked a young U.S. Special Forces captain training at CIGS to compare the courses.

"There is really no comparison," he says. "The U.S. Army course at Fort Sherman is geared towards the training of light infantry squads. It is shorter, lasting three weeks, and is planned to familiarize regular troops with the jungle. At CIGS, what you have is an instructor course for officers who will later pass this knowledge on to other units. The duration of the course is nine weeks and we know it is very tough. The depth of knowledge is very great."

There is an historical exchange between CIGS and the U.S. Jungle Warfare School in Panama, since CIGS was formed by Brazilian officers who had attended the U.S. Army school.

"This course is very famous in France," says the young legionnaire. "I am here to learn what my real limits are. When the course is over, I will be allowed to wear the CIGS emblem of the jaguar on my foreign legion uniform. People in the French army know what it is and what it means."

CIGS is the place where the brotherhood of Jungle Warriors is created. Those who have earned the emblem of the jaguar have learned to be resourceful, stealthy, and

effective hunters. Many will return to CIGS to become instructors. Some will be sent to border units to lead squads of men in the jungle, applying what they have learned. For Brazilian officers and NCOs, graduating from CIGS is one of the highest military honors they can attain. Regardless of their missions, however, the men know, when they leave the gates of the school and are greeted with the cry of *"Selva!"* by the guards, that the jungle will be a part of them forever.

When the course is over, the students are finally allowed to wear the "Jaguar Badge," one of the most coveted symbols in any army. They are now part of the select brotherhood of Jungle Warriors.

THE LITTLE SOLDIERS

The Jungle Infantary Battalions

At first sight of the young soldiers of the *Batalhão de Infantaria de Selva* (BIS), the Jungle Infantry Battalion, it is impossible not to feel amazed. In fact, the impression is that the unit is composed of boys in men's uniforms. Most are short, with boyish faces, light, almond-shaped eyes, and complexions like the Amazon Indians. When relaxed they joke, and are acutely curious in a shy, quiet way. It is hard to imagine these boys holding their own against fit, mature troops. But this first impression disappears upon entering the jungle, when, as if by magic, these young soldiers seem to grow tenfold.

They pace the nearly impassable jungle floor with silent movements. When asked to climb a tree for a drill, a young soldier negotiated almost 80 feet (25 meters) in a few seconds and descended head first. Morale is always high and joking recurs at every break in training. Since many, perhaps most, grew up hunting and fishing in the jungle, the only thing that really changes for them in the army is the prey. After my first outing with the troops of the BIS, I immediately understood the capabilities they possess.

Operations

There are two seasons in the Amazon region. The official manuals note that temperatures range from "equatorial," which is hot and extremely humid, to "subequatorial," which is hot and humid. Regardless of the definitions, the climate is hell-like all the time. In the winter, which lasts from January to June, there are strong rains. The summer brings soaring heat and less frequent, although equally torrential, rains. The damage done by these violent storms is enormous. Trees are scattered everywhere, their roots ripped from the ground. Lightning strikes can sometimes form whole clearings in the thick jungle.

The terrain of the Amazon is generally irregular. In the north, on the Brazil-Venezuela border, the jungle resembles the Vietnamese highlands, with some mountain ranges such as that containing the 9,650 foot (3,014 meter) Pico da Nebina, Brazil's highest peak, reaching close to 10,000 feet (3,000 meters). The nearby state of Roraima in Brazil has natural rolling plains, barren of trees. But this open land is the exception in a mostly homogenous region of tropical jungle. The high ground is light reddish clay, while the low grounds and river banks are fine white sand. Both types of soil are very susceptible to erosion where tree cover has been removed.

Rivers, lakes, and small river arms, called *igarapés,* are everywhere, providing abundant fresh water and acting as natural barriers. The seasons change the terrain incredibly. The areas that are dry in summer can be under water in winter. The locals build special log flats for their cattle when the low pasturelands are submerged. Cows are kept floating on these log flats under stilt houses for

(Previous spread) *Soldiers from the First* Batalhão de Infantaria de Selva *(BIS), the Jungle Infantry Battalion. These "little warriors" of Indian stock are naturals in the jungles of the Amazon, where most of them grew up.* **(Facing Page)** *Tradition lingers on even in the distant Amazon.* **(Above)** *"Cuca," the mascot at the First BIS base, strides among soldiers returning from patrol. Her presence helps to remind the men of the power of the jungle.*

First BIS company badges. These young soldiers consider their units to be "the best in the world" and compete among themselves to see which unit is the most efficient. **(Facing page)** A local BIS trooper holds a quati, a distant Brazilian relative of the raccoon. Although generally aggressive and tricky, these carnivores behave gently with the soldiers.

the winter and are fed by hand until summer. Certain areas, known as the *igapós*, are in reality submerged jungle. The river rises so high that only the crowns of the tallest trees appear above the surface, creating a giant underwater forest—truly breathtaking, but a tactical nightmare for military forces.

The jungle itself can be either primary, with large trees growing in alternate layers greatly inhibiting passage, with visibility rarely exceeding 90 feet (28 meters) vertically as well as horizontally; or secondary, made up of a dense mixture of thickets, bushes, thorns, lianas, vines, and brambles, where passage is exceptionally difficult and visibility is reduced to no more than 30 feet (9 meters).

With visibility impaired, a soldier has to rely on other senses to achieve surprise and superiority in the jungle. Sounds are perhaps the most important indication of enemy presence, so the soldier must have very acute hearing. An ax cutting down trees, machetes opening trails, the cutting of a branch or a vine, leaves falling on water, rotten wood being stepped on, weapons being cocked—all of these sounds are taken into account by soldiers on patrol. Certain birds, such as the *seringueiro*, or "rubber tapper," make calls that alert the forest to impending danger. The soldiers at BIS also rely on finely honed tracking skills in order to "read" the jungle. Through footsteps, broken twigs, or the direction of bent foliage, a soldier can usually tell with accuracy what the current situation is around him.

Marching through the jungle is generally the only way to arrive unseen at an objective. A well-trained squad marches ten hours a day in the bush, resting frequently for the jungle drains so much energy that often a patrol will need to recover from an excessive march in order to engage the enemy. Firing zones are virtually useless in dense foliage. There are so many obstacles to stop or deflect a bullet that BIS soldiers quickly learn to build firing tunnels without disrupting plant cover. These cones of air are the only space through which the enemy can be hit. With poor visibility and the availability of cover at almost any point, combat inside the rain forest is usually undertaken by small groups that engage in very rapid firefights. A less experienced unit would most likely be devastated by the Jungle Warriors. If not hit in the initial confrontation, the enemy would be followed and harassed until completely annihilated.

Jungle combat doctrine dictates that it is sometimes better to wound a man than to kill him. The sights and sounds of a wounded soldier can create feelings of desperation in a squad. A terrified enemy becomes easy prey as training gives way to instinct and instinct in the jungle usually loses out to facility and experience. A few, well-trained men are more valuable than large numbers of soldiers in the jungle.

(Above) *In the Amazon one is always wet, be it from the rain, sweat, or the rivers.* **(Right)** *Like most Amazon units, the First BIS serves its community by maintaining a small, well-kept school.*

other than the grenade itself. Heavy weapons are of little use in the jungle, although they are essential for guarding jungle bases and open areas. Usually a platoon will carry a 7.62mm FN MAG GPMG (general purpose machine gun) for covering fire, as well as some form of grenade launcher for bunkers and tunnels.

Packs are smaller than average, designed to carry only the most important equipment. Jungle boots are lighter than their more orthodox counterparts, with hard soles (stainless steel in times of war) and a webbed body for easy water drainage. Headgear is as light as possible, usually a cap or the traditional CIGS bush hat, called the *bandeirante* in honor of the seventeenth century pioneers who braved the jungles of Brazil's interior. The hard, metal helmets used in the jungles during World War II not only were extremely heavy, but hindered one's ability to hear. A jungle knife, or machete, is the inseparable companion of the Jungle Warrior, and is more often at hand than in its sheath.

It is, however, the soldier's experience in jungle combat that will be his most important weapon. Combat in the Amazon is completely different from combat in other areas and is rare in the jungle proper. With few exceptions, airfields, roads, villages, rivers, and any point of entry or exit to the jungle are where most battles occur. These are predictable contact points and their domination will probably result in control of the entire area.

In order to defend an area, the army builds jungle combat bases: simple, yet heavily defended areas from which both defensive and offensive patrols can be launched. These bases insure control over neighboring

Because of the hardships encountered when crossing jungle terrain and the need for agility and flexibility when confronting the enemy, Jungle Warriors need specialized equipment. The Brazilian army uses the locally made paratrooper version of the Belgian FN FAL 7.62mm rifle with folding stock, a light, easy-to-clean, rugged, and water-resistant weapon with power and range. It also doubles as a simplified grenade launcher, requiring no extra weight

civilian settlements by conducting "hearts-and-minds" campaigns to win the loyalty and friendship of the locals as well as to gain control of a vast area of jungle. Since there can be no fixed lines of combat in a rain forest, a base has to be defended from all sides. Fields of fire are built around the base with heavy, as well as light, weapons positions. Alarms, ranging from rudimentary wires and cans to sophisticated infrared and electronic devices, are installed in key areas. Outward-facing spotlights are added for night fighting. Mines are laid where they can stop an assault, and patrols are prepared for both reconnaissance and ambush. The objective is to create layers of defense, hopefully trapping the attacking force as far out as possible, from the compound, inflicting as much damage as possible, and thereby breaking the attack. An enemy on the run is much easier to kill, especially when he has been exposed.

Towards the Border

The infrastructure of the BIS Jungle Infantry Battalion guarantees a constant influx of highly trained jungle troops. While officers are prepared at CIGS, the men are trained at battalion level and transferred to areas of need. The First BIS, located in Manaus, is the foundation from which practically all new units are formed and sent to the border. Slowly, the Brazilian army has begun settling remote areas, territories where white men have practically never been and where new Indian tribes are occasionally found. Important units are now located in unknown and exotic places like Querarí, Iauaretê, Itaituba, Tabatinga, Japurá, Uauaris, Surucucu, Maturacá, Humaita, and São Gabriel da Cachoeira. These units employ the same doctrine and training as at the First BIS.

When emergencies occur, the border troops, as well as the units in Manaus, go on alert. More often than not, units of the First BIS are airlifted to strengthen the border garrisons. Forward units can be on the scene in any part of the Amazon in twelve hours or less. The close working relationship of the air force and navy accounts for a short reaction time of twenty-four hours, excellent for such a large and difficult territory.

Rigorous jungle training at CIGS, combined with constant training and deployment of the "little soldiers" of Brazil's jungle infantry battalions, has resulted in the growth of an army of jungle experts, able to survive, fight, and organize civilians into regional militias if needed. The philosophy is one of learning the local ways and relying as little as possible on outside supplies without losing combat effectiveness. In the unlikely event that the Amazon is invaded, the Brazilian army would be able to transform itself into a large guerrilla force, using the jungle with deadly efficiency. Currently, however, the Brazilian army faces the daunting task of defending its vast Amazon borders against very real enemies in a series of low intensity confrontations. The motto of the First BIS states it well in a simple, colloquial way, *"O que vier nós traça!"* — "Come what may, we'll handle it!"

(Previous spread) *Lt. Col. Paulo César Freitas de Oliveira, the young commander of the First BIS, on a solo recon of a stretch of river where his troops will conduct maneuvers. He is the perfect man for this unit, with jungle, paratroop, and special forces training. His leadership is shown by the high morale his men display.* **(Above)** *Handling the MAG 7.62mm GPMG.* **(Left)** *Not all is action and roughing it.* **(Facing page)** *Rappelling infiltrates a squad into the canopy from a Pantera helicopter.*

FIRE ON THE BORDER

Special Frontier Battalions

February 26, 1991, 1200 hours. The dark brown waters of the Traíra River slither like an oily python over the boulders breaking its surface. Every few hundred meters, considerable rapids show that the river is one to be reckoned with. Deep, secondary jungle lines its banks, leaves and branches occasionally dropping into the flow, littering the brown waters. It rains, lightly at first, then intermittently stronger. The jungle is otherwise quiet.

At a spot where the Traíra slowly horseshoes is an abandoned mining camp called "Vila Esperança." A seventeen-man detachment from the Third *Pelotão Especial de Fronteira* (PEF), Third Special Frontier Platoon, relaxes in an improvised mess hall at the camp. Two Colombian gold miners have been captured in Brazilian territory and are awaiting the chopper that will ferry them across the border to Colombian authorities. They have offered to prepare a special Colombian dish for the soldiers; the atmosphere is friendly and calm.

Suddenly gunfire shatters the jungle silence. It comes from the far bank of the river, some 65 feet (20 meters) away in Colombian territory. Three sentries posted on the river bank are killed first with expertly placed shots. The soldiers in the mess jump from their seats and sprint in the direction of the firing, just as more gunfire erupts from the jungle fringe on both north and south. The ensuing fusillade leaves nine Brazilian soldiers wounded, along with the two Colombian prisoners. In moments, the firefight is over.

A force of forty well-armed guerrillas, thirty-eight men and two women, have taken the camp. Approaching the

soldiers, many of them in intense pain, the guerrillas identify themselves as members of the *Fuerzas Armadas Revolucionárias de Colombia* (FARC), the "Colombian Revolutionary Armed Forces," Simon Bolivar Command, Force and Peace Faction. They ask for the highest ranking officer and are surprised to see Lt. Frederico Augusto Pinto de Freitas assume responsibility over his men, bleeding profusely and barely able to stand. They carry an assortment of weapons, ranging from hunting rifles to 5.56mm sub-machine guns. Approaching the mortally wounded Colombian prisoners, they ask if they have been mistreated by the Brazilian forces. The two men are able to answer negatively before perishing. The guerrillas take eighteen Para-FAL rifles, two radio sets, some uniforms, and other assorted equipment. As swiftly as they appeared, they disappear down the river, taking along the detachment's boats.

Action and Reaction

The attack at Vila Esperança had been meticulously planned and executed. Marksmen positioned themselves on the facing bank as an effective frontal firebase, while two assault groups arrived down river from the north, crossing into Brazilian territory just upstream from the camp. One group then moved to the edge of the forest on the northern flank, while the other swung through the jungle to prepare an attack from the south. It was clear the group had extensive military training.

(Previous spread) *BEF troops charge from a Pantera helicopter. Stretches that may take a few days on foot or by boat can be covered in minutes by chopper.* **(Facing page top)** *Gate guard at the First BEF base in Tabatinga.* **(This page top)** *A patrol moves into the hot jungle.* **(Above)** *"Brazil begins here..."* **(Right)** *Two troopers relax on the Letícia-Tabatinga border.*

(**Previous spread**) *Daily routine at the BEF base. A squad prepares for patrol while Cesar the base mascot greets a friend.* (**Above**) *There is more than one war going on in the Amazon. Well-balanced meals are provided for abandoned children at the border schools.*

With the guerrillas gone and few supplies left, the soldiers at Vila Esperança had literally been left to die. To travel the 62 miles (100 kilometers) to Vila Bittencourt, the closest army base, would take anywhere from three to five days. The Traíra is a powerful river, and two waterfalls present formidable obstacles, since to circumvent them boats have to be taken off the water and manhandled across the jungle.

Immediately the detachment's medical officer, Lt. Renildo Sergio Batista dos Anjos, himself wounded, began operating on the most serious cases. With few supplies available, he managed to perform several important lifesaving measures, without which the number of casualties would have been much higher. Luckily, the replacement detachment arrived at the scene three days later and was able to call in reinforcements and evacuate the dead and wounded.

Three nights later, while Brazil learned about the daring attack on the news, Lt. Col. Evandro Pamplona Vaz was already at the head of his First *Batalhão Especial de Fronteira* (BEF), Special Frontier Battalion troops combing the jungle in hot pursuit of the guerrillas. Other units were rapidly being mobilized and sent to the area. After

a well-planned search, one of the Brazilian patrols came upon the Colombian guerrillas. Like lightning they struck in a brief but intense attack. Seven guerrillas were left dead on the jungle floor, while others ran for their lives. A few rifles, Brazilian uniforms, and other pieces of equipment were found with the dead. Two days after a shocked country first learned of the attack, news came of the swift response, with assurances that other action would follow. The hunt by the Brazilian and Colombian military was on.

The area around the Traíra mountain range was declared off limits to all but military personnel. A frontline air base was set up in a few days, and more than twenty aircraft began operating from Vila Bittencourt. The navy sent the river patrol ship, *Raposo Tavares,* on a sweep up the western Amazon River to establish an important supply and communications base on the Japurá River, as well as to strengthen security in the area.

Extensive reconnaissance and data-collecting missions began to turn out important corollary information about drug laboratories and river-crossing points between Colombian and Brazilian territory. A vast area barely inhabited by man was now being turned inside out.

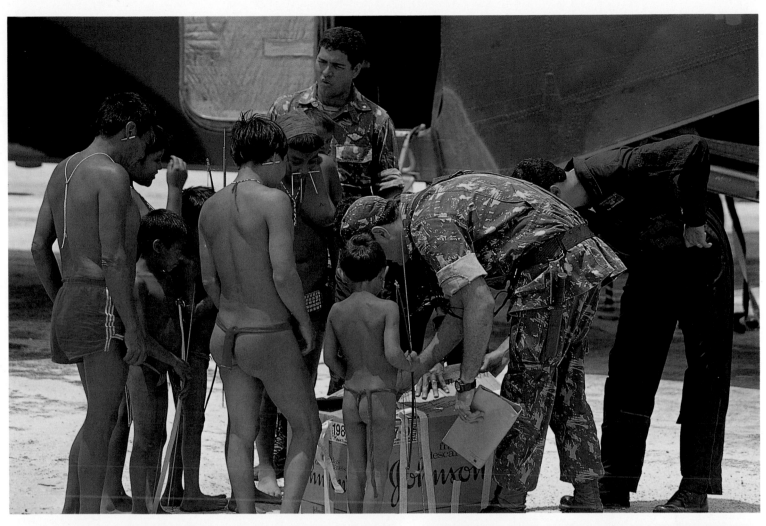

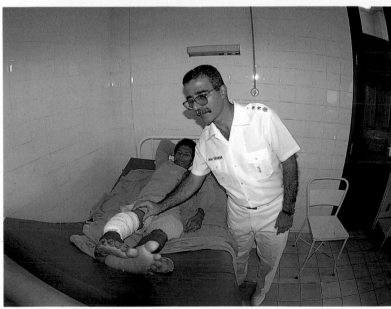

The army, navy, and air force provide most of the relief to the needy people of the borders. **(Top)** Air force pilots and army lieutenants bring modern supplies to the Yanomami. **(Bottom left)** An army doctor checks a Ticuna elder who had been bitten by a poisonous jararaca snake. **(Bottom right)** These doctors often treat cholera cases on the Peruvian and Colombian borders.

Well-prepared and combat-proven, BEF troops are on constant alert along the northern borders of Brazil.

Although most of the information about the Traíra River incident remains classified, it is clear that the Brazilian military quickly established firm control in the area. The camp at Vila Esperança was transformed into a jungle combat base and became a hive of activity.

"My men were mad, really mad," said Lieutenant Colonel Vaz after the operation. "They wanted those guerrillas more than anything." Further details have been withheld in order to protect the security of current operations. While the Traíra River incident was not the first to require a concentration of specialized troops in the border area of Brazil, it was the first incident where the entire country realized the importance of safeguarding the remote Amazon border from a clear and present danger.

Analysis of an Attack

What prompted such a daring attack by the FARC? The answer is complex. The Traíra mountain range on the Brazilian-Colombian border is rich in newly discovered gold. On the Colombian side of the border, across the Traíra River, sit the gold-mining settlements of Puerto Nuevo and Garimpito. Here, a transient, heavily armed population ranging from two thousand to five thousand gold prospectors mingles with guerrillas and powerful drug cartel members seeking refuge in the jungle. Puerto Nuevo and Garimpito are virtually devoid of government control; gold and drugs serve as currency. These settlements are located only 3 miles (5 kilometers) from the Brazilian border.

On the northern banks of the Traíra River, in Colombia, gold can only be found underground. Such mining requires the use of explosives. The Colombian government, however, in an attempt to reduce hit-and-run attacks by guerrillas against military and civilian installations, has forbidden the use of explosives in the area. Unable to purchase or use

explosives legally, the Colombian miners flock to the Brazilian side of the Traíra, where alluvium gold is abundant. With only a prospecting pan and patience, a miner can find enough gold to make a fortune.

  · North of Vila Esperança on the Traíra River, entering the Castanho *igarapé* (river arm), lies the Tucano Indian area known as Pari Cachoeira III colony, which is protected by the Brazilian government. This region is also very rich in gold, as is the area of the Macu Indians to the south of the Traíra Mountains. Vila Esperança served as the central camp for the large Brazilian firm, *Companhia Mineradora Paranapanema,* which in agreement with both the Tucano and Macu tribes, mined gold in the region in exchange for royalties. Protected by only a tiny contingent of Amazon state policemen, Vila Esperança was constantly subjected to harassment and blackmail by gold miners and guerrillas from the Colombian side of the border. The miners offered gold in exchange for protection and undisturbed access to Brazilian territories; the guerrillas needed gold to purchase arms and food, and so a strong alliance was struck. With guerrilla protection, Colombian gold miners often took boatloads of supplies, utensils, and even women to trade with the Tucano Indians. At the same time, large drug cartels were using the jungles of the region to hide processing laboratories and to provide alternative border-crossing points to the traditional northern drug routes.

After several years, in 1990, *Paranapanema* gave up and handed over control of the Vila Esperança camp to the Brazilian army. Troops immediately began operations. Hundreds of Colombians were captured in Brazilian territory and returned to Colombian authorities. Constant patrols made the local drug traffickers weary, as did the surveillance and interdiction of drug traffic at important points on the rivers.

The unrelenting pressure by Brazilian authorities on the Colombian elements culminated in the February 26, 1991, attack by FARC. It seems unlikely that the group considered the long-term implications the assault would have.

The Brazilian army, long aware of the magnitude of defending such a large and hostile border was finally able to evaluate the results of the *Calha Norte* plan to settle the border region through a network of combined military-civilian outposts along the Amazon perimeter. Had the Traíra attack occurred ten years earlier, logistical problems would have made response to the incident far less effective.

The *Calha Norte* project was implemented in 1985 with the following objectives: to increase the presence of Brazilian authority on the border, to make government institutions and services available where previously they were lacking, to create incentives for trade and good diplomatic relations with neighboring countries, and to ensure the general protection of the Indian and local populations, as well as the integrity of Brazil's territory. In reality, the settlements created by the *Calha Norte* plan are modern-day jungle versions of nineteenth-century U.S. Cavalry forts on the Great Plains or French foreign legion outposts in the North African desert.

Brazil Begins Here

Tabatinga is a small city on the banks of the Solimões, as the Amazon is locally called on its course from the Andes to Manaus. Right next to Tabatinga, on the Colombian side of the border, lies Leticia, a sprawling port city. It is in Tabatinga that the First BEF has its headquarters.

We arrive at the small, well-equipped airport on a regular commercial flight from Manaus. The terminal is immaculately clean and functional, quite frankly a surprise in such a remote place. The streets of the town are spotless. A multitude of young children in neatly pressed uniforms gathers around the local school, and we have to remind ourselves how far we are from the closest urban center.

Just past a bend in the road, a white, freshly painted wall with the inscription "Brazil begins here" signals the First BEF's headquarters. A beautiful, hand-carved wooden plaque, made by the local Indians, depicts the head of a jaguar and hangs just below the sentry box at the main gate. Jungle Warriors' home.

The tranquil, idyllic image of the town gives way to reality as Lieutenant Colonel Vaz and a BEF captain tour the compound with us. A guerrilla group of considerable size has just been spotted no further than 9 miles (15 kilometers) from Tabatinga, across the border in Colombian territory. Troops of the First BEF were constantly rotating in and out of the jungle and the tension was apparent in each soldier's face. Incursions by drug dealers from across the border had also forced the battalion to assume police duty. Just a few weeks earlier there had been an attempt to kidnap the local manager of Brazil's state bank, *Banco do Brasil.* The kidnapping failed, but people are nervous. The BEF officers show great concern each time Lieutenant Colonel Vaz must drive over the border for meetings with Colombian authorities. The officers fear an attempt will be made on his life; they relax only when he is back in the compound. BEF soldiers have the distinctive look and the cat-like movements of men who have seen combat. Although they are young men not too long out of school, they are already veterans of hundreds of tense jungle patrols.

Behind the main buildings of the base lies a vast jungle training area separated by an obstacle course and firing range. Brand new Pantera (Aerospatiale SA-365 Dauphin) and Esquilo (Aerospatiale AS-350 Ecurreil "Squirrel") helicopters, French-designed aircraft assembled in Brazil, fill the grassy space under the watchful eyes of their mechanics. The jungle humidity can wreak havoc on these machines. To the left, a young *maracaja* cat, similar to the ocelot, is strung by his leash to a pole. The captain walks in the direction where the cat is lying, yet not too near.

"Careful, this guy is tricky and dangerous," he says with a grin. Playful squirrel monkeys run up the captain's leg and perch on his shoulders, but they jump off as he approaches another resident of the BEF compound. Cesar,

(Facing page) *The army's engineering battalions, spread throughout the vast Amazon basin, have been responsible for an impressive series of roads and dams that have made life better for isolated settlements. Indians, disease, rains, floods, erosion, and the impenetrable jungle have not stopped these men from completing their mission.* **(This page)** *This painting, which hangs on a wall at the Boa Vista Engineering Battalion headquarters, depicts Amazon military engineers at work.*

a large, fully grown jaguar basks in the sun while a patrol prepares its packs and equipment for a sortie. The soldiers seem to enjoy his presence, although he serves as a constant reminder of their destination.

The atmosphere of the BEF base is highly professional, yet we discover that the military aspects of the garrison are not the only mission these men expect of themselves. Most of the people of Tabatinga are poor and undernourished. A center for study and training, built and tended by the battalion, teaches needy, abandoned children a series of skills, including handicrafts, agriculture, and animal husbandry.

The town has two schools, clean, well-kept, and very active. Many of the teachers are wives of men from the garrison. Their children mingle with the native children, learning the ways of the local tribes. A young boy tells us one of the Indian girls had come to school wearing a scarf, because every hair had been pulled from her head. The Ticuna Indians perform this ceremony each time a young girl steps into womanhood, she had explained to her schoolmates. Lieutenant Colonel Vaz often visits the schools, making sure things are shipshape, sometimes organizing weekends in the jungle in order to teach the children the survival techniques at which his soldiers excel.

Tabatinga's hospital, also run by the army, is another example of the benefits the military units bring to the border region. Long lines form every morning in front of the hospital, which is staffed entirely by army medics. Many of the patients belong to the Ticuna tribe living just outside the village. The hospital provides the only medical attention available in the region for a very needy population. As would be expected, snakebites are a common sight at the Tabatinga hospital. More broadly threatening is an outbreak of cholera in the Colombian, Peruvian, and Brazilian territories of the Amazon. The disease has already taken a heavy toll. But the hard work of military doctors who, along with civilian institutions, go on cholera patrols to improve hygiene and sanitation in the region, seems to have controlled the disease, at least near Tabatinga. Earning regular military pay, the army doctors at this outpost know how useful they are to the population and have very high morale.

In Tabatinga the army is aware of the importance of every bit of stone and mortar that make up the structure of society. When the local Portuguese-speaking radio station lost its two disc jockeys; lured by life in the big cities of the South, rather than see his town depend upon Spanish-speaking Colombian radio for news and entertainment, Lieutenant Colonel Vaz pulled occasional "duty" as a D.J. to make sure that the station stayed on the air!

Roads, although few, are well paved, and construction occurs all over town, many times provided by the Battalion

Lt. Col. Evandro Pamplona Vaz, commander of the First BEF.

itself. The lampposts in Tabatinga are painted with the Brazilian green and yellow of the flag, evoking great pride. Few men have served as best man to as many grooms, or godfather to as many babies, as Lieutenant Colonel Vaz and the commanders of other border outposts across the Amazon. We left Tabatinga knowing we had witnessed history, the settling of a country. It was clear that the army and its related forces were essential institutions in this remote region. The war against poverty, ignorance, and malnutrition will be long and strenuous, but in Tabatinga we saw that it was already being waged.

The Gold Rush

Within the vast confines of the Amazon lives the majority of Brazil's 220,000 Indians. Of that number, an estimated 15,000 comprise isolated, primitive tribes who have had little or no contact with white men. They are hunter-gatherers with absolutely no knowledge of the world outside the jungle. The other tribes live at various levels of assimilation into modern culture, wear Western clothes, use modern tools and utensils, speak Portuguese in various forms, and believe in the Christian faith. Brazil has set apart 469 Indian reservations, some 220 million acres (89.5 million hectares), making it among all countries the one that best protects its indigenous populations. This huge land mass, mostly in the Amazon, equals one and a half times the state of Texas, or four Great Britains. Each Indian in Brazil is allotted almost 1000 acres (400 hectares). In the United States, by contrast, reservation lands provide 50 acres (20 hectares) per capita.

Only recently has the vast mineral potential of some of the Indian areas been unearthed. On Brazil's borders with Colombia and Peru in the troublesome Traíra region, and in the highlands of Roraima, known as *Cabeça do Cachorro,* the "Dog's Head," bordering Venezuela, great mineral riches have been found.

The state of Pará in the eastern half of the Amazon region is the site of two of the most promising hopes for Brazil's economy. In 1967, a Brazilian geologist was forced to land his helicopter in the Carajás Mountains. There he found remarkably pure iron ore, as well as several other minerals. With further study, the Brazilian government discovered that the Carajás region contained some of the richest mineral deposits in the world.

The Carajás deposits of gold, copper, manganese, bauxite, nickel, tin, and a series of other minerals prompted the building of the Tucurui Dam, which not only supplies energy to a large mining operation but to cities, towns, and villages in the area as well.

The other large mining operation in the state of Pará is known as *Serra Pelada,* "the Naked Hills." About a decade ago, when the earth under a tree felled during a storm was found to contain gold-laden rocks, a massive gold rush began. Three years later, Serra Pelada had already produced over $800 million in gold. The sight of the immense Serra Pelada mine is breathtaking, as thousands of men clad in nothing more than clay-covered shorts march up ladders, into holes and terraces like ants, busy at their daily chores. The largest gold nugget in history, weighing 80 pounds (36 kilograms), was found at Serra Pelada, along with other legends in the annals of gold mining.

The mine continues to produce at the same levels as ten years ago, and there seems to be no near end to the amount of gold on the site. The discovery at Serra Pelada, however, was the starting point for the hundreds of smaller gold rushes that are occurring all over the Amazon. Large mining companies, as well as individual miners with small boats, outboard motors, and prospecting pans, charge into the jungle, many times entering Indian territory. It is extremely hard to keep prospectors away from sites, given the number of miners involved and the potential for such vast wealth. Clandestine landing strips carved out of the forest, river camps, forays by foot into the jungle, and even dredges and flats with suction hoses are being brought into the area by a veritable army of fortune seekers.

With the Indians as *de facto* owners of the land, and no other institution able to control the Indian boundaries, the Brazilian military is called on to perform an endless and frustrating task.

It is estimated that the Indian territories contain $50 billion worth of mineral resources. A developing nation with a large underprivileged population must tap into these riches. There is mounting pressure on the Brazilian government, however, to preserve all Indian ancestral lands as reservations. Some groups have even gone so far as to propose the creation of a separate Indian nation in the recently designated Yanomami area, which comprises large portions of Brazilian and Venezuelan territory. Supporters of the idea wish to transform the 23.5 million acre (9.4 million hectare) area granted recently by the Brazilian government into a sovereign nation for the thirty-six hundred (some anthropologists say there may be up to ten thousand*) Yanomami Indians of the region. With borders difficult to patrol and impossible to limit with physical barriers, the result of the creation of such a state could well be the extinction of the Yanomami and other tribes by prospectors, drug traffickers, and disease.

Missions representing different branches of the Catholic and Protestant churches have entered into the debate. National and international environmental groups have emerged as voices supporting the rights of Brazil's Indians hopeful that their fate will be different from that of the indigenous populations of other countries. An interesting aspect of this heated debate is that no one seems to have asked the tribes themselves what they believe is best for them. In the meantime, the only practical means of protection arrives in the form of army platoons assigned to the areas adjacent to Indian regions. Supplies and medicines come on air force transports and helicopters, the only aircraft that brave dangerous flights into uncharted jungle for other than financial gain.

While large numbers of miners are extracted from the Indian regions, the army seems to be fighting a losing battle against men intent on mining the gold of the Amazon. Moreover, Indians like the Yanomami of the "Dog's Head" region, or the Macus on the Colombian border, migrate over international boundaries. Even if protected on one side of the border, they can be in danger on the other. There is no way to ensure full protection until these tribes begin to participate as citizens in the social structure of the countries where they live.

Cocaine World

The Indians of the Amazon are extremely vulnerable to drug cartels and guerrilla groups active in the region.

Information concerning the exact number of Yanomami Indians in Brazil and Venezuela varies greatly. Many reports include the populations counted in both countries, and due to constant cross-border migrations of the several tribes, it is possible that many individuals have been counted two or more times. What is known, however, is that there are four major branches of the Yanomami tribe. They speak different languages and often indulge in warfare among themselves. The numbers above are the estimates which have appeared most frequently in the press and on government documents.

The Macu Indians hunt with blowguns and poisoned arrows, drawing on the jungle for their livelihood. However, they move over *epadu* territory. This Amazonian plant, similar to the coca plant, is used by drug traffickers to produce cocaine paste. This "poor man's coke," although not as sought after as the coca plant from the Andean foothills, is hidden by the jungle canopy and grows in profusion. One *epadu* plant can be harvested four times a year and produces for over ten years. The Macu Indians have been manipulated by the cartels of the Uaupés River area to grow and transport *epadu* leaves. The leaves are taken by boat or small plane to heavily guarded laboratories hidden in the jungle. In 1987 alone, the Brazilian police destroyed over five million *epadu* plants in Macu territory. While many tribes consume a variety of hallucinogenic drugs for medical or ritual purposes, they are now being introduced to new forms of processed drugs produced for profit by the region's underworld.

Cocaine, produced in greater and greater quantities in Brazil's northern neighbors, will probably cause the most serious low-intensity conflicts in the region over the next decade. Used for hundreds of years by the Incas and their Quechua descendants in Peru and Bolivia, who chew its leaves to reduce the effects of hunger, cold, and altitude, the coca plant also has legal uses, including the production of medical anesthetics and as one of the ingredients for, Coca-Cola, the soft drink which takes some of its flavor from coca leaves after the harmful alkaloids have been extracted.

It is when dried coca leaves are mixed with kerosene and sulfuric acid that they become a problem to most governments. In Peru and Bolivia, this process produces cocaine paste, a yellowish-white residue similar to plaster. The paste is then sent to Colombia, where it is refined into cocaine. Guarded by heavily armed men who often have been trained by foreign mercenaries, these vast laboratories, hidden deep in the Colombian jungle, process the drug to be shipped to major buying markets in the United States and Europe.

About two hundred kilograms of coca leaves produce about one kilo of refined cocaine. For harvested leaves, the peasants of the Andes can receive up to $2,000, a fortune for most workers in the region. One kilo of cocaine in the United States, sometimes "cut" to raise profit, can reach a price of $150,000 on the streets.

The governments of Colombia, Peru, and Bolivia have attempted to reduce the production of cocaine by introducing other crops that would supplant cocaine as a source of revenue in regions where up to 90 percent of the population is involved in the business. The U.S. has tackled the problem by sending agents to South America to combat production. Blackhawk helicopters, night-vision goggles, modern rifles and machine guns, electronic and satellite surveillance, and other intelligence-gathering equipment have been brought to bear in the region. For many observers, the invasion of Panama and the arrest of Manuel Noriega signaled the beginning of true drug wars against the cocaine cartels.

In Brazil, some laboratories and *epadu* plantations have been located and destroyed. But with the noose tightening on the cartels in Colombia, many operations began moving into the deep Brazilian jungle, establishing a looping route through Venezuela and the Guyanas toward Europe, where cocaine attains even higher street prices than in the U.S. Often legitimate commercial routes are used to smuggle the drug south to the cities and ports of Brazil. The Amazon River is also used to transport the drug to Manaus and Belém. The vast size of the country makes this trade extremely difficult to counter. Although the Brazilian army, military, and air force have rapidly improved intelligence-gathering centers and techniques, the actual strikes against the drug cartels are the responsibility of Brazil's federal police. In many cases, these men act on intelligence provided by military sources and often use army, air force, and navy transportation to carry out their strikes. The military in the Amazon knows, however, that the conflict is in grave danger of escalating and that the consequences in all of Latin America may be grave.

Danger to the Peoples of the Forest

Brazil's Indians walk a tightrope over the abyss of progress. Many of the voices who clamor for their protection in their current state are in fact condemning them to extinction. In the Traíra River region, where gold is easily found in the shallow rivers, fighting between prospectors and Indians is frequent and fierce. "You never cross or outwit an Indian," a gold prospector told me. "He will never forget your face or the sound of your name until he kills you." The distrust is mutual; it seems to be practically impossible to control violence between prospectors and the native tribes. The Tucano Indians of Pari Cachoeira III are an example of a tribe that has been allowed to adapt to the modern world at its own pace, rather than having institutions impose change. The Tucanos have been granted rights over the gold in their region and defend it against any intruder. They seem to want progress, respect the international borders, and shun all contact with missionary groups. Of all the Indian tribes in the northern borders, they appear to be the most prosperous.

The Caiapós of the southern Amazon have transformed their tribe into a cooperative farm. They are reaping the benefits of progress, boasting a standard of living higher than that of most Brazilians. They plant and trade with the use of tractors and trucks. In the evening, satellite

Scenes from the border: army patrols see constant activity; a Ticuna village, where fishing is the primary source of food; Yanomami children from the village of Uauaris, on the Venezuelan border.

dishes silhouetted against the jungle canopy show the results of their labor.

Aggressive tribes like the Corubas and Matis, who live in almost total seclusion in the Javari Valley along the Peruvian border, have killed several whites attempting contact. Since oil is suspected to exist in the area, the resilience of these tribes will soon be tested, if not by Brazilian oil companies, then surely by the growing Peruvian guerrilla movements such as the *Sendero Luminoso* ("Shining Path") and *Tupac Amaru* Revolutionary Movement, that, if pressed by the government in Lima, may see the Coruba and Mati territory as a safe haven.

The future of the Indian tribes in Brazil is a subject of great complexity and emotion. It is clear that the Brazilian military represents the most effective stabilizing force in the region currently. Already protected by Brazil's army, navy, and air force, however, the tribes ultimately must be assimilated into society, earning the same benefits it provides its citizens, otherwise they will be unable to hold back progress, even with protection. Such is the situation in this volatile and remote corner of the world.

For Those Who Died

The night before we left Tabatinga, Lieutenant Colonel Vaz took us out for dinner then showed us a group of clean, simple concrete houses on a small Tabatinga street, far from the center of Brazil. The houses had been built with funds donated by the soldiers in the battalion for the families of the men who had died at Vila Esperança. Lieutenant Colonel Vaz had waited to show us this simple memorial until the last evening of our stay. We left town the next day deeply impressed by what we had seen. The army seemed to know how to keep the fire on the border under control.

Gold prospectors just off an FAB Buffalo from Roraima's far north are handed over to federal police agents at Boa Vista airport. Many of these men eventually will try to return to the jungles of the Yanomami.

83

PATROLLING THE RIVER SEA

The Amazon Flotilla

River warfare is not new to the Brazilian navy. In 1865, reacting to provocations by Paraguayan president Solano Lopes, Brazil, Argentina, and Uruguay signed a war pact against the mighty Paraguayan forces, beginning a bloody, four-year conflict known as "The War of the Triple Alliance," or simply the "Paraguay War." After a naval blockade of the Plate River (an estuary of the central South American Paraguay River basin), the Brazilian fleet, then the only one of the three allies able to go head on with Paraguay's navy, began to force its way slowly upriver.

At the Battle of Riachuelo, on June 11, 1865, in a large-scale naval confrontation that was to define the future of the war, the Brazilian navy succeeded in defeating the enemy, forcing a retreat that included a series of tough stands by both Paraguayan naval and land forces in several parts of the river. The Battle of Riachuelo is probably the largest battle ever to be fought on inland waterways. It taught the Brazilian navy the tactical importance of effectively patrolling and maintaining its vast river systems.

The Amazon River is also known as the "River Sea" due to its enormous dimensions. Its basin provides about twenty percent of the world's fresh water. Its tributaries reach into the whole of northern South America; at least ten of these tributaries are larger than the Mississippi River. Many of the streams have never been navigated by white men, and vast tracts of the surrounding jungle have never been explored.

The Amazon has an average depth of 90 feet (28 meters) and is navigable — by all except the largest ships — from its mouth, guarded by the Marajó Island, a tropical paradise roughly the size of Denmark, to the Peruvian jungle port of Iquitos. From Manaus, the sprawling capital of the state of Amazonas and the central point in the region, it can still take a week to navigate to the Peruvian border.

With the exception of a few major cities and industrial sites, the banks of most rivers in the region are sparsely populated, composed mainly of wild secondary jungle or marsh land. According to Jacques Cousteau, who conducted detailed experiments in the Amazon basin, these rivers have a wider variety of fish than the Atlantic Ocean. Their waters teem with large alligators, dolphins (both the gray and the Amazon pink), sharks, swordfish, rays, giant turtles, anacondas, eels, the *pirarucu* — the largest freshwater fish alive, measuring up to 15 feet (5 meters) and weighing as much as 500 pounds (225 kilograms), — the infamous piranha, and large manatees (known locally as *peixe-boi,* or "bull fish").

The rivers of the Amazon are sometimes used to move illegal cargoes, such as contraband drugs, gold, animal hides, and wood. In order to patrol this vast area and provide an effective link to all corners of the river network, the Brazilian navy must maintain a powerful fleet, with a constant presence on practically every river.

Operating from major bases at Manaus and Belém, the navy employs both large and small craft specially designed for river navigation and warfare and is capable of displaying water, land, and air strength — if the situation demands it — in an impressive show of coordinated force. The navy's ships also support both the army and the air force in daily operations. In no other military region in Brazil do the armed forces operate with such well-orchestrated use of joint force as in the Amazon, where obstacles imposed by the terrain demand cohesive military effort.

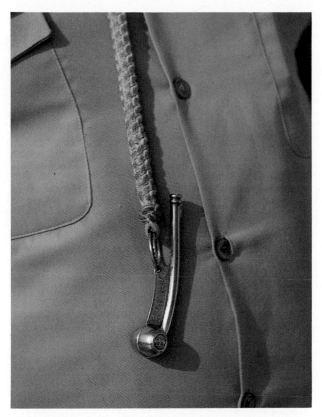

(Previous spread) *A navy Esquilo approaches* Pedro Teixeira *for a "meeting of the waters" landing.* (Facing page) *FLOTAM's commander arrives at the base.* (This page) *Brazil has a strong river warfare history, dating from the 1865 "War of the Triple Alliance," when Brazilian and Paraguayan naval units clashed in the waters of the Paraguay River basin in central South America.*

Though wild and hostile, the rivers of the Amazon are busily trafficked by craft of different shapes and sizes — from the tiny dugout canoes that resemble nut shells, known by the *caboclos* (locals) as *montarias,* or "mounts," to the large freighters that cautiously negotiate the changing river. The most common form of transport is the "motor," a boat approximately 30 feet (9 meters) long, with a main covered deck usually crowded with people sleeping in hammocks alongside crates of bananas, fish, tools, and other assorted gear.

These craft cruise the rivers performing a multitude of tasks. Some serve as transportation links for remote river locations. In others, vagrant salesmen peddle cheap goods, missionaries supply their missions, or fishermen hunt for abundant waters. The navy, along with the local port authority, keeps check of these vessels and their activities, but more search patrols are needed to control the flow of goods through the Amazon.

The Amazon poses dangers and surprises nonexistent in other areas of the world. The massive convergence of the waters of the Amazon with the Atlantic Ocean causes the phenomenon of the *pororoca,* a tidal bore characterized by a giant broken wave several feet high that roars upriver, consuming everything in its path. Smaller, yet powerful, waves follow in its wake, destroying large sections of the shoreline. Sand and sediment, when carried downriver, are deposited suddenly in unexpected places, blocking large segments of the river.

Primitive boats that use the Amazon River and its tributaries as their major roads pose threats to larger ships. When asked what he dreaded most on the river, Comdr. Paulo Roberto Baldner, skipper of the river patrol ship, *Raposo Tavares,* answers without hesitation, "My worst nightmares are of local barges which are pushed by 'motors' and are sometimes totally unpredictable. On one occasion such a boat was pushing hundreds of logs around a river bend and lost control of its cargo, scattering tree-size logs across our bow. It required emergency procedures to avoid badly damaging the ship. The fact that this occurred at night only made matters worse." Many of the smaller craft, he added, are required to use maritime traffic procedures but often act in unpredictable ways — such as substituting the official red and green navigation lights for orange, purple, and blue lights that are more to their liking — requiring the complete attention of the bridge crew on larger ships.

The Fleet

In a combat situation, the river is vulnerable to attack either from the jungle or from the air. Defensive countermeasures must be constantly practiced. Several techniques have been studied and passed on by generations of sailors. As on other rivers of the world, vessels sail upstream as close to the banks as possible, where the water flows more slowly; sailing downstream, they navigate midstream, to make use of the maximum flow of water. The Amazon, however, has snags and vegetation that pose special problems.

"We know a few tricks that come with living and working here," says Comdr. José Heitor Macedo Ribeiro Pereira, skipper of the navy hospital ship, *Carlos Chagas.* "We sometimes use changing water flows at river bends to 'slingshot' the boat around certain areas, increasing our speed momentarily. We also know where and when to cross certain rivers, and what the condition of the basin will be at various times of the year. It takes trial and error as well as data that may have taken years to amass until you finally understand these waters. River operations are very different from open ocean missions."

In Belém, navy corvettes and coastal patrol boats police the mouth of the Amazon, a strategic position since colonial days when Portuguese vessels fought pirates to acquire control of the region. During World War II, Brazilian naval and air bases were of important strategic value to Allied aircraft and convoys because of their position facing the coast of Africa. Belém was important not only as a

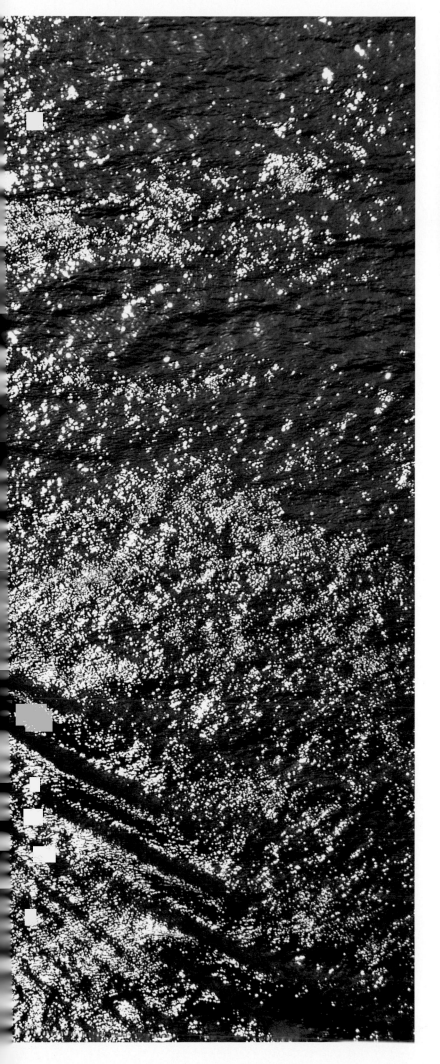

(Facing) *Na Pa Flu* Raposo Tavares *glides along a silver river. The helicopter hangar and landing deck are visible, as is one of the fast-assault landing craft on the stern.* (Above) *The navy hospital ship* Carlos Chagas *looms in the background as the medical emergency launch returns from a patrol.*

(Above) *Helicopters enhance the offensive capabilities of the Amazon fleet — from full aerial attacks to recon, medevac, commando insertion, cargo transport, and service between ships.* **(Facing page)** *Pedro Teixeira cruises from the Negro River into the Solimões.*

Pedro Teixeira *in position on the Amazon River. The large NaPaFlus*
of the Amazon Flotilla can coordinate the defense of a vast area
with land, air, and river parties.

source of rubber, wood, and other goods that supported the war effort, but also as a base for warships and aircraft on submarine picket duty. To this day, the Brazilian navy patrols the northern coastline and the mouth of the Amazon from its base in Belém.

Upriver in Manaus, on the slopes of the Manaus-Porto Velho road, lies the headquarters of the *Flotilha do Amazonas* (FLOTAM), the Amazon Flotilla, where most of the special river patrol boats are based. The port is near the confluence of the Negro and Solimões rivers, the site of an unusual and beautiful natural phenomenon. The waters of the Negro, black with decomposing leaves, meet the caramel-colored waters of the Solimões, laden with nutrients and sediment from its western origin. The two rivers converge without mixing and flow alongside each other for almost 20 miles (30 kilometers), before the waters blend into a solid tan color, and the river is finally called Amazonas.

From FLOTAM headquarters one can watch the *Pedro Teixeira* class naval patrol ships and the *Oswaldo Cruz* class hospital ships prepare to set sail. *Pedro Teixeira* and its sister ship *Raposo Tavares* are the largest and most powerful naval patrol vessels in all of the Amazon and are very different from seagoing military vessels.

Designed and built in the huge Rio de Janeiro Navy Arsenal, they were constructed to act as powerful forward bases from which combined operations can be launched with fast, effective results. The sleek, light gray ships, numbered P20 and P21, measure about 200 feet (62 meters) and displace seven hundred tons at full load. Powered by two 3,849 horsepower diesel engines, they can reach a speed of sixteen knots and have a shallow 5.4-foot (1.65-meter) draft for less drag on the mostly calm river waters. A main turret on the bow holds a 40mm gun, and a series of positions amidships and at the stern pack mortars and machine guns.

These ships house a hangar and flight deck and can store, service, and operate their own Esquilo helicopters, which are armed with a variety of rockets, machine guns, and missiles. The vessels can also serve as forward platforms for air force and army helicopters. Modern, effective, and comfortable, the *Pedro Teixeira* and the *Raposo Tavares* contain an array of advanced electronic equipment that would astound the seventeenth century Brazilian explorers of the Amazon for whom the vessels are named. With few landing options available in the jungle, these ships sometimes become emergency helipads. At thirteen knots, they have a 5,000 mile (8,000 kilometer) combat radius and can reach almost any point in the Amazon river system.

Aft of the flight deck, *Pedro Teixeira* and *Raposo Tavares* carry smaller vessels, including two landing craft for a force of marines. At any location, these ships can attack with naval bombardment, with heliborne attacks, or with commando-style marine operations. In an area of potential low-intensity warfare, the presence of such offensive capabilities is of utmost importance.

During the Traíra emergency, the *Raposo Tavares*, on patrol in the western Amazon, was rapidly diverted to the Japurá River, where it launched several heliborne reconnaissance missions, provided protection for the settlement of Vila Bittencourt, and served as an effective communications and air traffic control base. Not all of its missions were made public, but it is known that the ship was critical to the large army and air force operations in the area.

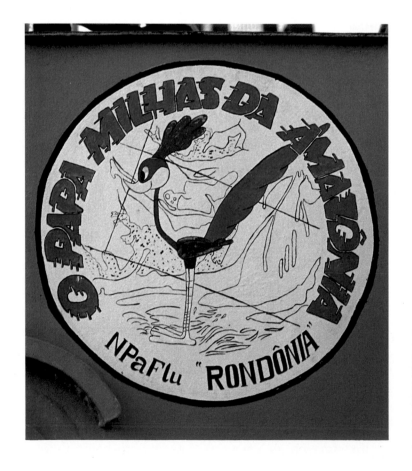

The smaller NaPaFlus of the Roraima *class offer an alternative in shallower rivers. These fast boats concentrate the same firepower as larger boats. The Amazon Flotilla is the strongest river navy in the region, perhaps the world.* **(Above)** *The "Roadrunner of the Amazon" shows the competitive spirit of NaPaFlu Roraima's crew.*

In September and October, the rains that fall on the eastern slopes of the southern Peruvian and Bolivian Andes, as well as on the Brazilian central plains, begin filling the right bank tributaries of the Amazon. These rivers reach capacity in February and March, just as the rains begin in the Guyana highlands and in the spur of the Andes, feeding the tributaries of the left bank. These overflow waters reach the main channel of the Amazon in April, May, and June, when the level of water in the right bank tributaries begins to drop. June is the month when the Amazon River crests, but the natural balance of rainfall feeding into its tributaries reduces the potential destruction of its floodwaters.

Because this constant variation occurs in water level in the Amazon basin, as well as in several small, hard-to-reach lakes and marshes, the Brazilian navy also utilizes the smaller *Roraima*-class river patrol boats, which are named after three of the states in the Amazon — Roraima, Rondônia, and Amapá. With a draft of 4.2 feet (1.28 meters), measuring 150 feet (45 meters), and displacing 364 tons fully loaded, the vessels are fast, going where the larger ships cannot. Surprisingly high superstructures enable them to carry substantial armament, in addition to two landing craft. Built in Brazil, these gunboats carry almost as much firepower as the larger *Raposo Tavares* and *Pedro Teixeira,* but with better range and flexibility.

The Ships of Hope

Brazil also utilizes its Amazon Flotilla for purposes other than combat. Because of scarce resources and the medical problems of an impoverished and malnourished population, the navy ships are transformed into "ships of hope." They transport large units of navy medics and support government programs that bring relief to these needy people. Teachers, social workers, even missionaries ride with the navy patrol boats as they sail deep into unknown areas, fighting a war against disease and malnutrition.

The missions of the two naval hospital ships, *Oswaldo Cruz* and *Carlos Chagas,* are very important. Named after two Brazilian physicians who discovered the cures for yellow fever and trypanosomiasis (Chagas disease), tropical diseases that heavily afflicted Brazil, these ships are the only source of medical aid for the people who live along the river banks of the Amazon basin.

Crewed by young medical officers, these 155 foot (45 meter) floating hospitals are eagerly awaited by families in the deep jungle interior. Esquilo helicopters airlift emergencies to hospitals and fly doctors to villages to attend to urgent cases. Small houses on stilts, isolated from major villages and settlements, often light fires or fly pieces of blankets or clothing to signal the ships, known

A Roraima-class river patrol ship on the immense Amazon River.
The clean and comfortable ships offer an oasis of civilization amidst
the most primitive surroundings on earth.

(Facing page) *The most impressive characteristic of the Amazon River ships is their ability to navigate very shallow waters.* (Above) *Local "motors" provide most of the transportation in the basin.*

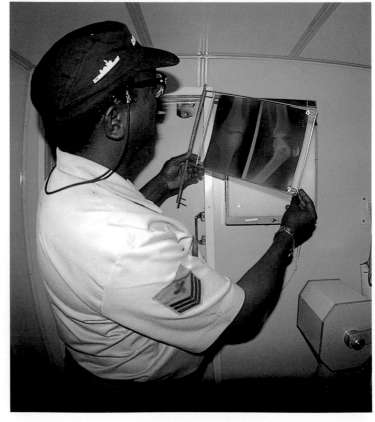

(Previous spread) *The hospital ship* Carlos Chagas *is one of the "ships of hope," taking medical services to the far reaches of the Amazon basin. Known as the "white ship with the red cross" by the locals, this floating hospital is in reality a warship against poverty.* **(This page top)** *Advance medical parties scout the shores ahead of the ship and take care of non-emergency situations.* **(Bottom)** *The ship has complete x-ray facilities.*

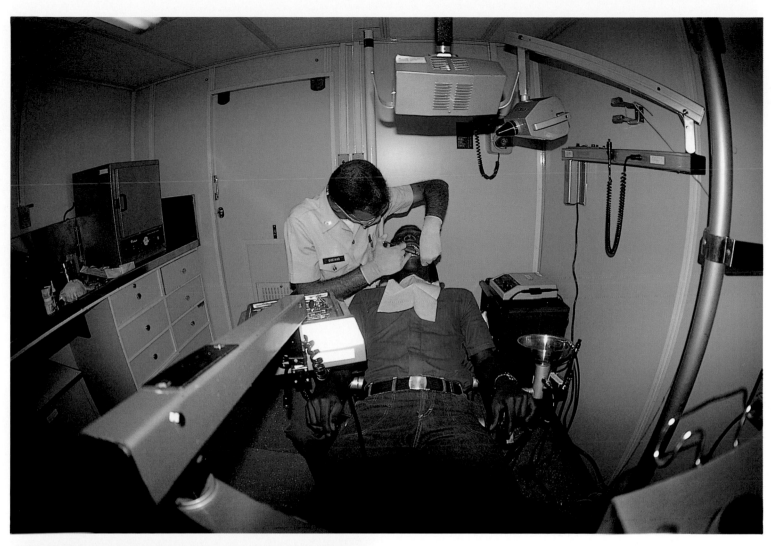

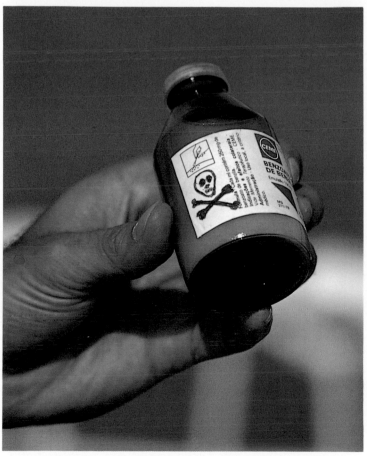

(Top) Navy doctors and dentists perform countless surgeries during a normal day. (Bottom) Sometimes, doctors must invent warnings for normally harmless medication, as the ignorance of some of the villagers has prompted them to take a full bottle of medicine in order to get well sooner!

to the locals as the "white ships with the red cross," as they approach.

Usually, fast motor launches with a small crew of medics, orderlies, and pilots are sent ahead to make assessments and treat any non-emergency situations. If conditions are critical, a helicopter will be summoned. Both ships are equipped with a dental office, recovery areas, and laboratories with modern equipment capable of performing practically any type of operation, including major surgery.

Living conditions for people who make their home along the rivers are terribly primitive. The local diet consists of *mandioca* (cassava) — roasted and ground to rid it of poisonous hydrocyanic acid — fish, bananas, and avocado, as well as an occasional jungle animal. Most houses in the area are built with walls facing the river to block the view from passing boats, while the jungle-facing side is open to insects, bats, and snakes that may be deadly. Stings from river rays as well as snake, piranha, and alligator bites are not uncommon. Less frequently, victims of jaguar attacks are treated.

"On one occasion, a man who had been bitten by an alligator and had lost a leg paddled all night to reach the ship," the chief dentist aboard the *Carlos Chagas* tells us. "Unfortunately, he died after we began treatment. We were his only hope and what kept him alive so long."

Hygiene conditions are terrible; sometimes water used for cooking and drinking is the same as that used for sewage purposes. The child mortality rate is high, life expectancy is low, and diseases that in any other place would be considered harmless can require emergency procedures.

"If you look at one of these people, man or woman, you generally see a very fit middle-aged person," says one of the doctors. "However, you may be surprised. A lady who appeared to be about fifty-five years old was paddling her small dugout at nearly the speed of the ship. I was impressed by her powerful rowing. When she came aboard and I asked her age, I found out she was only in her thirties."

Typical diseases include malaria, hepatitis, several types of tapeworms, skin diseases, gastroenteritis, parasitosis, urinary infections, tuberculosis, and several dental problems. It is common in these regions to treat patients from outside the borders of Brazil. With a recent cholera outbreak in Peru and Colombia, the navy sent its ships into the upper Solimões (Amazon) to work with Peruvian and Colombian authorities.

According to Commander Heitor, "This is a quiet, yet necessary mission. The men who serve on our ship are aware of how important our mission is. When the white ships arrive, in reality what is arriving is the twentieth century."

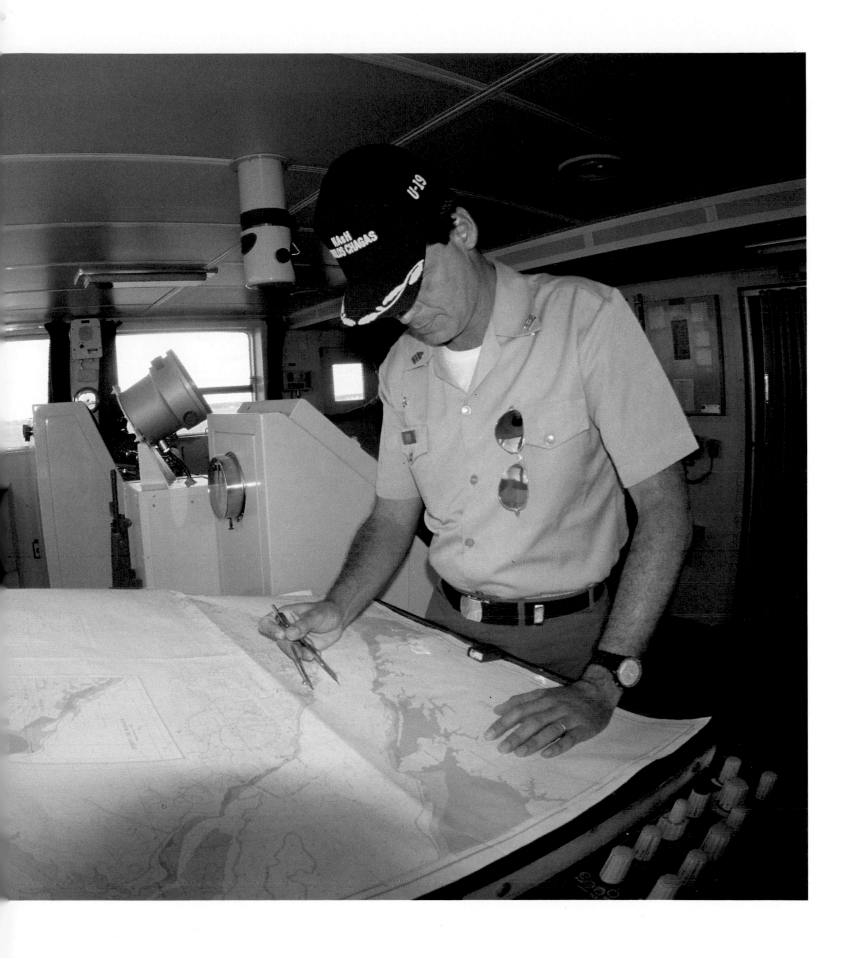

The skipper of the Carlos Chagas, Comdr. José Heitor Macedo Ribeiro Pereira, plots the ship's position from the bridge. Navigation on the rivers of the region is tough and requires experience, much of which is passed along by each generation of sailors.

The navy has its own (Fuzileiros Navais) naval fusiliers or marines, capable in jungle, in air, and in river warfare operations. Their main mission is to act as an embarked strike force, giving each NaPaFlu its own infantry arm. The marines are one of Brazil's truly elite forces.

Jungle Marines

The small marine detachments based in Belém and Manaus comprise another important branch of the Brazilian navy. These elite troops are well-trained in jungle warfare, river landing operations, small squad combat, and commando-style warfare.

Called *fuzileiros navais,* or "naval riflemen," the marines can operate from a floating base or from land, using small vessels as well as navy helicopters. In many places, the fastest access is by river. As soon as one of the river patrol boats arrives on the scene, its marine contingent can land either to attack an area or to hold a defensive position until heavier forces arrive.

These soldiers are well-equipped with Para-FAL 7.62mm rifles, MAG machine guns, and Taurus/Beretta submachine guns. Their uniforms are different from their army counterparts only in the lighter camouflage color, more suitable for fighting on the river banks than in the dark jungle interior.

Although the task of completely controlling the waterways of the Amazon is impossible, the Brazilian navy makes its presence effective. It defends strategic areas and launches devastating offensive operations, as well as coordinating strikes with army and air force units. It uses its ships to create remote river bases that would normally take months to establish. And its river gunboats still perform the noblest task of all, bringing relief to the people they defend.

The marines are accustomed to fighting wet. Their equipment, although similar to the army's, is geared for combat close to the river banks and in marshy areas. When asked to name the greatest danger in the Amazon waters, a marine jokingly remembered the candiru, a tiny fish that will penetrate any orifice exposed when swimming. Once inside, the fish opens its spine-like fins, causing excruciating pain.

The marines have their own
bases and training centers.
Their doctrine revolves
around small squad tactics.
(Top) Instructors generally
have CIGS training.

The marines in the Amazon are extremely effective along the marshy edges of the jungle. They perform special operations missions similar to the U.S. Navy SEALs and Britain's SBS (Special Boat Squadron). **(Top)** A submerged cable is used to cross an igarapé. **(Bottom)** Small squads of well-trained troops can cause unbelievable damage in the jungle.

Marines prepare to land from the Raposo Tavares *far up one of the Negro River's tributaries. Although proficient in small squad tactics, the marines are also capable of operating large-scale attacks and landings, complete with their own artillery and armored battalions, which are based throughout Brazil.*

FLYING WITH THE PARROTS

Visually Over The River

Dawn comes lazily in the thick, oppressive heat of Manaus. It is still dark, but ground crewmen are loading up one of the three C-115 Buffalos that form the flight line. Crates of all sizes share the tarmac with fuel barrels and a small tractor. In one of the wooden crates is a big hog that grunts and squeals loudly as the first rays of the sun reach into the jungle.

With the cargo aboard, the airplane provides no space other than two rows of red harness seats squeezed between the boxes and the airplane's inner walls. The load masters line up the passengers before boarding and give detailed safety instructions. The first few *urubus*, Brazilian black vultures, glide and circle over the main runway to the east, awaiting the heat of the sun. Soon there will be hundreds of the birds.

With all passengers aboard, the large, twin-engined, squat-looking beast whines to life and slowly turns onto the deserted taxiway. Minutes later, sitting on the end of the runway, the Buffalo unleashes the energy of its twin General Electric engines and accelerates into the sky. Immediately after takeoff, the pilot veers the plane to one side to avoid several vultures already crowding the airspace.

As the C-115 turns to the north, white smoke like the vapor from dry ice floods the hold. It is condensation from the air conditioner. The passengers are sweating profusely. We all try to ignore the stench of the nervous pig and a few smaller creatures that are pets.

After a couple of hours and a short stop at Boa Vista, the small capital of the state of Roraima, we reload a similar cargo and take off again. Twenty minutes later the flat, rolling fields of Roraima give way to dense jungle.

The pilots follow a snaky brown river for a while, then suddenly they drop down to treetop level, while the river flows out of sight to the north. I look out the window at the ocean of trees. Endless, undulating, menacing, the trees rush by just below the aircraft. I can't avoid a terrifying thought. There is absolutely no place to land. Stories I had heard about the tension of flying over the jungle suddenly become very real. The only way to fly over this area, I think to myself, is to trust those GE engines, point your nose in the right direction, and fly on.

To make matters worse, I can't locate any landmarks. Knowing that the Buffalos do not carry advanced navigational equipment, I wonder how the pilot and crew will find their way across this monotonous green ocean. I walk to the cockpit. There, the pilot holds the stick while his "2P" (co-pilot) looks out his window. He has a large black-and-white aerial photo on his lap. A river comes up from the north, then snakes to the west. Perhaps it was the same one I noted earlier. On its surface are several small flatboats with light blue sheets of plastic serving as makeshift roofs.

"*Garimpeiros*," the crewmen tell me, gold prospectors in a forbidden area. Further ahead, the Buffalo flies over a large, bright orange rectangle cut into the jungle carpet. The pilot drops the left wing, and we can clearly see the enormous illegal jungle airstrip. A small settlement lies next to it.

As we fly on, I concentrate on details of the dense forest to relieve the tension. I can spot purple and yellow specks of the *ipê* trees, and occasionally, Brazil-nut trees, the towering *castanheiros* that overlook all others in the jungle. Like me, Maj. Antonio Carlos Moretti Bermudez

(Previous spread) *From the cockpit of an FAB C-130, the vastness of the jungle is quite apparent. Modern electronic navigational aids allow the Hercules pilots to relax over the rain forest.* **(Above)** *A C-115 Buffalo comes in on its nose-down "crash approach." These planes can land on football fields.*

With only the rivers as a guide and impoverished people awaiting aid, flying the Buffalo over the rain forest requires a special type of pilot.

118

is on his first border flight, and he is mesmerized by the beauty of the trees.

Suddenly, the jungle rises sharply up at us! The trees pass a mere thirty feet under the wing. Parrots and other birds fly in all directions as the "Buff" powers overhead. The speed of this seemingly cumbersome plane is clearly evident as the treetops race desperately underneath. Then, as suddenly as it rose up, the jungle falls away. We have just passed over the first of the mountain ranges that line the path to our destination. The jungle here reaches an altitude of 9,000 feet (2,600 meters). A cool mist swirls through the trees below. Our pilots keep the nose of the Buffalo as close to the mountains as possible. They point out the "woman's breast," the "anvil," and several other landmarks in the mountain range.

A wide mesa appears below the nose, and the "Buff" sweeps in on a warning pass to clear the runway. We have reached our destination right on time and circle for final approach. The plane's nose takes a frighteningly exaggerated dip as the propellers momentarily shift into idle. In this strange, nosedown position the props assume a different slant. The "Buff" continues in this "controlled-crash" attitude until the clay and gravel runway appears beneath the undercarriage. The nose comes up, the wheels bang violently, and reverse is immediately engaged. We stop so quickly that it feels as though we have just made an aircraft carrier landing with arresting cable in the middle of the jungle!

I look out the window and see a small man and three young boys waving happily. They are practically naked and hold bows and arrows. I suddenly remember where we have landed. As the cargo ramp lowers with its mechanical growl and the load masters prepare to disembark passengers and cargo, Major Bermudez grins at me and says, "Welcome to Yanomami country."

We step out into the frantic unloading and immediate preparation for the trip back. The engines are kept turning and the pilots seem eager to take off. At Surucucu, this distant garrison at the top of Brazil, cold mists often veil the mountains and the jungle in a dense, ethereal fog. It is common for flights to land and find themselves trapped by the mist, so the pilot and crew want to save time on the ground. The Indians seem at ease with the soldiers and airmen gathered around the plane, which serves as a beacon of strong curiosity. Some of the Indians speak broken Portuguese words and phrases. Gifts are exchanged and I truly wonder whether the Indians prefer their lives to ours, but before I can orient myself, it is time to board. With the Yanomami waving good-bye, the ramp closes. The engines roar to life and the sturdy Buffalo takes off, its nose pointing back to Boa Vista, and more supplies.

(Above) *A clandestine runway in northern Roraima.*
(Bottom) *To the miners, Amazon gold is the only hope for a better life.*

(Top) *Prospectors prepare to board an FAB plane which will evacuate them from Indian territory. Soon, however, most will be back. The war against illegal mining is tough and sometimes futile.* **(Bottom)** *Aircraft parked at Boa Vista airport. These planes support myriad gold mining and drug-running operations on the northern border.*

The Brazilian Air Force performs a series of missions in the Amazon skies. Besides the Hercules, Buffalo, and Bandeirantes of transport command, other aircraft fly special missions on a routine basis. This Gates Learjet is used for photo reconnaissance.

We climb to 9,000 feet (2,600 meters). This time the flying is not as tense, though every bit as dangerous. Now the pilot can use a VHF beacon to locate the general direction of Boa Vista. I ask the pilot and crew a few questions about navigating in the forest and we compare the Buffalo to other transports in the *Força Aérea Brasileira* (FAB), the Brazilian Air Force.

"The Hercules has a series of electronic navigational advantages, such as the Omega, VOR, and ILS systems," says the young co-pilot now in control of the plane. "Yet when you fly over the Amazon, you have very few ground coordinates anyway. We are flying like it was done in the old days."

I ask the men how they navigate. The pilot, now in the right-hand seat, smiles and says, "Here in the Amazon we like to say we fly 'VOR.' For us, that means 'Visually over the river!'"

On the approach to Boa Vista the jungle gives way to the rolling plains of central Roraima. Leaving the jungle for this open land I feel instantly relieved. It is like the relief I felt seeing sky finally emerge beyond the depths of jungle canopy. I had truly learned how heavy the pressure of the rain forest can be on nerves and mind. But already I was eager to reload and head north again to fly with the parrots!

To Defend and To Integrate

The FAB has been a driving force in the pioneering and settling of the Amazon region. Flying dangerous missions into remote Indian, missionary, and military settlements, isolated villages, and special project sites, the Brazilian air force has come to know intimately the skies of this vast jungle, perhaps the most forbidding airspace on earth, other than the sky over the polar ice caps.

The distances between airstrips, the lack of electronic navigational aids, the dense forest canopy—all mean that a malfunction or miscalculation can prove to be deadly. Rivers provide the only alternative in case an airplane must be ditched. Living through a crash landing in an Amazon river is but the first tough step in survival, however. From Cruzeiro do Sul in the western Amazon state of Acre to Belém in the east is a distance equivalent to that between the northeastern Brazilian coast and Portugal, that is, across the whole of the Atlantic Ocean.

Given these vast distances and the dense jungle itself, the airplane provides the only means of transporting cargo to remote places in short periods of time. The British Chindits pioneered the techniques of aerial supply with the Royal Air Force in the Burmese jungles of World War II. Employing the early lessons learned by the RAF, the FAB has been operating cargo missions in the Amazon for

decades, first with Douglas C-47 Dakotas and PBY Catalina "flying boats;" today with the C-130 Hercules and C-115 Buffalo.

Air force engineers are constantly at work, building longer and better airfields deeper in the jungle. The *Calha Norte* settlements covering the perimeter of Brazil's northwest border now accommodate the heavy C-130 Hercules, where just recently only smaller aircraft could land. A virtual air bridge of supplies, tractors, fuels, electronic equipment, medicine, ammunition, and people links the far-off settlements such as Querari, Cucui, Iauaretê, Maturacá and Uauaris to the industrial centers in the south of Brazil.

"The Amazon skies can be compared to the airspace over northern Canada," says Maj. Gen. Antonio Alberto de Toledo Lobato, FAB commander in the western Amazon. "In Canada, the enemy is ice. Here, it is the jungle. In both cases, pilots are flying over vast expanses with their hands on the stick and their noses glued to the windshield."

Major General Lobato is eloquent in his explanation of the importance of the missions his men fly. "All of the Amazon is inhabited—by poor, needy people—but inhabited nonetheless. And the only way supplies can reach all corners of the region is by air or by river. Roads were built, but the forest claimed them back. In the Traíra operations, supply took over six days by river, and twenty-five minutes by helicopter. You see the difference in those figures. In the Amazon, the air force is the modern-day wagon train."

Brazil can rapidly dispatch a powerful fighter force to the Amazon region in case of attack. From the northern bases of Fortaleza and Natal, from the central highlands, from airfields in the main jungle cities, or from select airfields hidden in the bush, large numbers of Xavante and Mirage fighters can operate. With Boeing KC-137s orbiting as fuel stations for Northrop F-5Es and Embraer AMX fighter bombers based in Brazil's southeast, forward control centers can be set up in remote parts of the jungle for perfect coordination with fighters in the air.

Amazon Air War

Massive aerial operations of the type witnessed in the Gulf War of 1991 would rarely occur over a vast jungle area. In the skies over Vietnam, Laos, and Cambodia, the United States Air Force learned how hard it is to use air power successfully in jungle terrain. Some estimates claim that of all ordnance fired over the jungles of Southeast Asia during the Vietnam War, only fifteen percent hit intended targets. Of course, strategic targets such as ports, air bases, railroad depots, oil refineries, and communication and control centers are harder to camouflage and are therefore easier targets to engage. But American air-

(Spread) *A Bandeirante is boarded at dawn for an early flight into the jungle. The assorted passengers include civilians, Indians, and nuns who live in remote missions.* (Right) *To "paint the seven" is the Portuguese equivalent of to "raise hell." This squadron's badge says, "We twist the snake to paint the seven in the Amazon."*

men in Southeast Asia were frequently forbidden to attack these high-profile targets, spending most of their time in a frustrating war against the jungle.

The USAF developed many "bush-beating" tactics and weapons, however. Defoliants, napalm, cluster bombs, air-dropped electronic sensors, "people sniffers," heavily armed helicopter gunships, and C-130 Hercules "Spectre" gunships with awesome firepower and night-fighting capability were used extensively. Nonetheless, the U.S. Air Force, Navy, Army, and Marines lost 8,588 aircraft to the enemy. Of those, 57.5 percent fell to AAA, 5.3 percent to SAM s, and only 2.1 percent to enemy MIGs. Antiaircraft fire once again became the major concern to western aerial strategists who until then worried mostly about missiles and MIGs. After the war, large efforts were made in the development of countermeasures to radar-guided antiaircraft batteries and missiles in order to recover aerial supremacy in the air wars to come.

The ease with which Iraqi tanks, missile sites, and AAA batteries were found and destroyed in the Gulf War demonstrates the importance of aerial supremacy in desert warfare. But in the jungle, results—even using the lessons of Vietnam and the new generation of "smart" weapons—would be very different. The tropical rain forest is still "guerrilla country." Small squad tactics prevail. Satellite reconnaissance and missile interception, techniques of supreme importance on open battlefields, are relatively ineffective in the jungle.

The FAB must concentrate its training on supply and interdiction missions to protect major objectives in the Amazon. The river itself is obviously an essential supply line. While it is impossible to control all traffic flowing down every tributary, large sectors can be sealed off and controlled through ground-air coordination. Defense for cities like Manaus and Belém, as well as for smaller settlements in every reach of the great river basin, must be planned. In practically every scenario, however, strategic targets and control centers can be rapidly transferred further into the jungle.

Although they are well-trained for large-scale jungle warfare with several exercises throughout the year, the people of the FAB know that the chances of engaging in a massive aerial campaign are slim. Brazil has a strong tradition of diplomacy; any border disputes are negotiated. The real threat lies in low-intensity conflicts that flare up along different areas of the border.

Crates

The airport in Boa Vista is one of the busiest in all of Brazil, hardly believable for such a small and remote city. Yet beyond Boa Vista lies an incredible number of

(Top left) *Badge of the First Squadron of the Ninth Transport Group These are the men who "fly with the parrots," as low-level flying is referred to by FAB pilots in the Amazon.* **(Facing)** *A Buffalo skims the trees.*

clandestine airstrips carved into the jungle. These strips, known as *caixotes,* or "crates," are serviced by a multitude of daredevil mercenary pilots with various levels of flying proficiency.

Some of the "crates" are clandestine airports with amazingly sophisticated infrastructures. Others are unbelievably primitive. On a flight over Roraima, I saw a small airstrip built *uphill* in thick trees, allowing no more than a meter of clearance on either side for the wingtips of a small plane. Erosion caused by torrential rains destroys large portions of these strips, and many landings result in crashes. Often these strips exist solely to service gold miners and drug traffickers.

"The gold miners are like ants," says Major General Lobato. "We fly in, evacuate hundreds of them, blow up the clandestine runways. But we have to be on it again, or they return with incredible speed."

So many small Cessna, Beechcraft, Piper, and Embraer aircraft fly in the region that it is virtually impossible to know which of these flights are legal and which are not. Authorities estimate that eighty percent of the flights in the northern Amazon region are for illegal purposes. With the lack of good radar cover over the central and northern basin, many aircraft simply file false flight plans then disappear under the limited radar coverage of the major airports. Large aircraft, like the old DC-3s or Con-

vairs, have been known to take off with full fuel tanks and distant flight plans filed only to return a few minutes later to be refueled!

To counter such makeshift refueling operations and the large number of aircraft in this clandestine fleet, the FAB needs electronic help. By developing a radar umbrella over the ten most important airports in the Amazon region, the FAB estimates that it would be able to stop ninety percent of illegal flights. With the use of airborne warning and control systems (AWACS), like the Boeing E-3A Sentry or the Grumman E-2C Hawkeye, the FAB would be even more effective. Such airplanes, however, are terribly expensive and beyond the current financial reach of FAB planners.

Flight Line

The FAB is by no means a wealthy air arm when compared to the USAF, the RAF, or the *Armée de l'Air.* It is, however, highly professional. Most aircraft in the FAB inventory are well-suited to Brazil's geographic and economic realities. A strong and inventive domestic industry provides many of the aircraft in use, such as the Bandeirante transports; the Brasília, Xingu, and CBA passenger types; the Tucano trainers; and the Xavante and AMX fighters. In the Amazon, the workhorses are the Embraer Bandeirante, a small, twin-engine transport; the Lockheed C-130 Hercules; and the DeHavilland Canada C-115 Buffalo, the remarkable STOL tactical transport.

The Buffalo—like the venerable Douglas C-47, also famous for its Amazon flights—is an airplane that has become a legend after going out of commercial production. Capable of landing on extremely short airstrips by slanting its propellers, the Buffalo has engines so powerful that it is able to move *backwards* on an airfield by reversing its props. On some tiny strips, this capability provides the only way the airplane can taxi to takeoff position without hitting trees with its wingtips.

Since DeHavilland has discontinued Canadian production of the Buffalo, the FAB has been looking for a successor. Thus far, no other aircraft approaches the capabilities of the "Buff" when it comes to jungle operations. Although many of the army garrisons in the "*Calha Norte*" now have advanced landing strips for C-130s and other larger planes, the romance of flying the Buffalo over the trees will remain an FAB tradition for a long time to come.

FAB C-95 Bandeirantes perform a series of missions in the Amazon, ranging from transport and aerial photography to providing passenger service where no commercial airline would dare fly. Cheap to operate and easy to maintain, the Bandeirante is probably the most common aircraft in the region.

(Facing page) Engines are constantly tuned in the rough Amazon heat. (Above) A Hercules flies over the waterways of the basin. (Right) Most air force pilots in the Amazon are young lieutenants and captains. The handgun is a mandatory part of a flight suit.

Delivery of the new Embraer/Alenia/Aermacchi AMX tactical fighter bomber, a state-of-the-art aircraft capable of delivering its weapons with pinpoint accuracy, has greatly improved the FAB's fighter and ground attack capability. Although the AMX is not based in the Amazon, aerial refueling with large tankers or the "buddy" system of refueling from similar aircraft enables the AMX to operate from forward bases in the region. The larger F-5Es and Mirage IIIs, the latter using Boeing or Hercules tankers, can also be transferred to one of the major attack bases in the Amazon for interception and ground attack. When the FAB opened its *São Gabriel da Cachoeira* runway in the central Amazon, an F-5E squadron from Canoas AFB in Brazil's southernmost state of Rio Grande do Sul, flew a direct nine-hour flight with three tanker rendezvous on the way. The Traíra emergency was of utmost importance to the FAB, since aircraft had to respond immediately to support army operations in the area. While full details have not been released to the public, the general feeling among FAB personnel is that the operation was highly successful.

Along with the Bell UH-1H Huey, Aerospatiale Esquilo, and Super Puma helicopters, Embraer T-27 Tucano training and counter-insurgency aircraft are of great importance to the region because they are capable of flying slower and more precise missions, similar to those flown by Douglas A-1 Skyraiders in Southeast Asia. These U.S. aircraft were employed in attacks against small enemy units, especially to rescue downed U.S. airmen, keeping the VC at bay until the arrival of rescue helicopters.

In the chaotic urban centers of southeast Brazil, few people even think about the fact that while they follow the routine of their daily lives, FAB pilots, mostly young lieutenants and captains, are skimming the jungle canopy in death-defying missions over the vast reaches of the Amazon, one of the last frontiers on earth. The motivation for these pilots and crewmen is both professional and moral.

"It is really interesting," Major Bermudez comments to me, "that a common trait of the pilots who have served in the Amazon, where the hardships are by no means small, is that most of them want to return. In the Amazon, these men see the need for their work, and that gives them great satisfaction."

A Distant Past

Our mission is to fly from the Venezuelan border to Boa Vista. The cargo on board this flight is a filthy band of gold miners the FAB is evacuating from Yanomami territory. Although many of the miners were frightened by the turbulence we encountered a few minutes earlier, most have fallen asleep to the drone of the Buffalo's engines. These men have been in the deep jungle for weeks.

The miners look haggard, and they smell. Two sit next to me, looking out the window at the vast jungle below. One holds a ragged note pad and a pencil. Every few minutes he draws or jots something down and quietly comments to his companion. I am unable to overcome my curiosity and ask them, in the same hushed tone, "Is it worth it?"

"Yeah, you can make yourself," answers the miner next to me. Intelligent and literate, he strikes me as being a middle-class professional rather than a desperate gold prospector who risks life and limb in forbidden jungle territory. Yet here he sits.

We talk about the Indians, the border, the army, and the air force, and what it is like to face the jungle. As we speak, he keeps looking out the window, jotting down his mysterious notes.

Suddenly I understand what he is doing. Every river bend, every mountain range, every clandestine airfield is being registered in his soiled notebook. He is mapping his way back! I am amazed, not only at his resourcefulness and navigational abilities but also at his resolve. I ask him the obvious.

"Do you plan on returning?" He doesn't even blink.

"As soon as we arrive in Boa Vista I'll start preparing for my trip back. I only have one purpose here." He smiles, and I smile back, finally understanding one of the profound truths of the Amazon. The air force knows the situation, knows that this miner will return to Yanomami territory, yet the FAB must do its job. I thank both men and move forward to the cockpit.

The sun is behind us, its light deepening the colors of the afternoon. The jungle glows greener than I have ever seen it. Occasionally a stream turns silver and twists furiously out of sight below us. I will be returning south soon. I look once more at the two young pilots flying the plane. They sip coffee and talk quietly. The pistols they carry under their arms are mere details in the afternoon quiet dominated by the slipstream and the rumble of the engines. It is just another workday for the Jungle Warriors all over the rain forest that spreads beneath me as far as the eye can see. My work in the Amazon is practically finished. I suddenly realize that days like this will soon be part of a distant, heroic, and forgotten past.

Fighters can reach the
Amazon on short notice,
refueling from huge Boeing
KC-137 tankers. These F-5E
fighters can also operate
attack sorties from Amazon
bases if need arises.

A Buffalo landing is a great event at the Indian village of Uauaris.
(Right) Young Yanomami are always curious when the "Great
Birds" come in from the skies.

Esquilo helicopters are the backbone of the Amazon chopper force. Easy to maintain, maneuverable, and versatile, they are found on practically every Amazon air base. **(Above)** Crew and special (PARA-SAR) Air Force Search and Rescue commandos debrief after a mission.

Rappelling is essential in the Amazon. Clearings can be rapidly cut in the bush for makeshift pads, and insertion of troops can be achieved in record time.

The Embraer/Alenia/Aermacchi AMX Tactical Fighter Bomber is fully computerized, with a high-tech weapons delivery system, and is capable of aerial refueling from tankers or from other AMX fighters. Its intelligent and versatile design enables it to perform surgical strikes in any part of the vast Brazilian territory. Recently introduced to service with the FAB, it promises to be the air force's most effective fighter well into the twenty-first century. **(Above)** Lt. Colonel Teomar Fonseca Quírico banks with his wingman close at hand.

No airplane in the world today can equal the Buffalo's (Short Takeoff and Landing) STOL envelope. Its amazing power makes it perfect for the primitive clay airstrips of the Amazon. **(Right)** Imaginative posters such as this one mark the flight roster for the month.

138

Although famous for its lush jungles, the Amazon has open regions as well. Here, a Buffalo flies over the natural plains of central Roraima.

It is very easy to discuss the Amazon's problems without having been there. It is difficult to live facing the hardshipos and dangers of the jungle without the tools of the modern world. The Brazilian Air Force works day and night to bring comfort and progress to those who live in the hostile world of the rain forest.